# Pasta Veloce

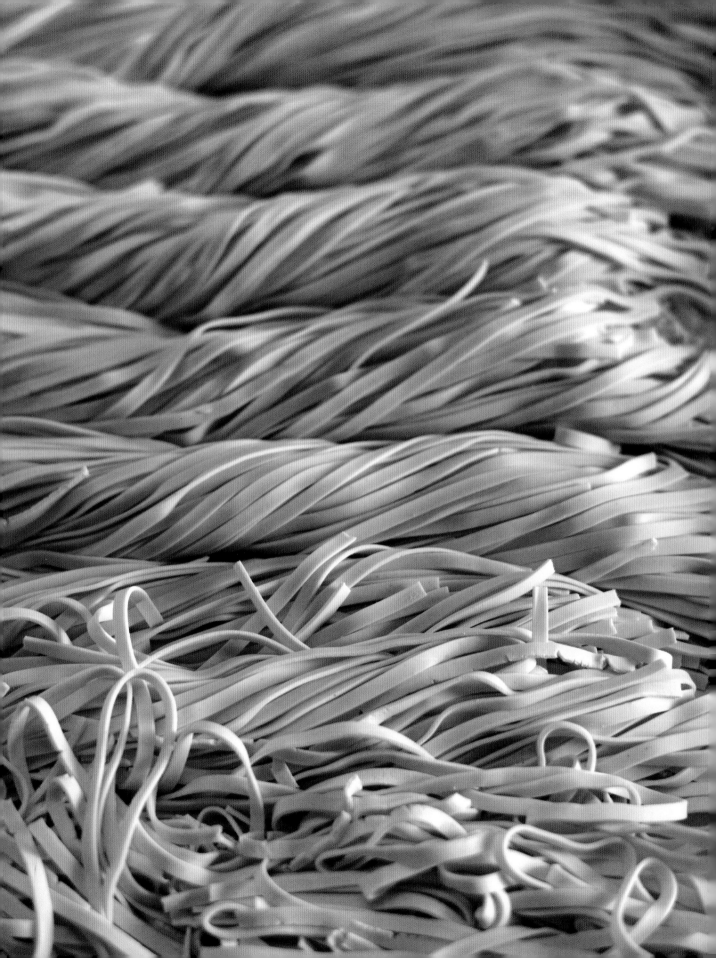

# Pasta Veloce

100 FAST AND IRRESISTIBLE RECIPES
FROM UNDER THE TUSCAN SUN

FRANCES MAYES
AND SUSAN WYLER

PHOTOGRAPHS BY
STEVEN ROTHFELD

Abrams, New York

# Contents

# Seafood 115

# Pestos 197

# Saluti!

Pasta's cardinal virtue? Speed! Many tasty dinners can be prepared in the time it takes to boil the water, throw in the salt, and cook the pasta to pleasing perfection. There are hundreds of slow pastas, but many, both contemporary and those derived from classic recipes, are *molto veloce*, very quick. Take the Roman favorite *cacio e pepe*. Toss pasta with pungent pecorino cheese, a generous blast of piquant black pepper, and a dollop of salty pasta water to smooth it all out. Presto! This classic is more than the sum of its simple parts.

Tuscan construction workers cook up a bowl of plain spaghetti on-site, which they dress at their makeshift table with olive oil and Parmigiano. Down-home food to generations of Tuscans is simply pasta topped with chopped tomatoes quickly sautéed with herbs, lots of herbs. Or when tomatoes reach their summer peak, skip the cooking and just stir in fresh diced tomatoes. Pestos, such as the old favorites of basil or walnuts, are made in a flash. A beyond-easy pasta is broccoli and *fonduta*, melted cheese with cream. A meal in a moment. From simple to elaborate, pasta is the most versatile food on earth.

These are rustic treasures, but quick pastas can attain elevated status, too. If you manage to score a truffle, nothing exceeds the pleasure of tagliolini mixed with good olive oil and graced with the thinnest shavings of aromatic

truffle. This book was conceived one night over a rich and irresistible lemon and pistachio linguine (page 79) served by my coauthor Susan at her house. We marveled over how simple it is to make, despite such a luxurious effect. Everyone at the table asked Susan for the recipe. Before we poured the last drop of wine, we'd decided to write this book.

Soon Susan and I were brainstorming over seafood, mushrooms, nuts, vegetables—all candidates for *pasta molto veloce*. We love improvising. A splash of wine, some lemon zest, a handful of herbed breadcrumbs and you have something divine on your plate. We had great fun collaborating and inventing as well as perfecting tried-and-true pasta favorites.

Many Italians eat pasta every day—sometimes twice a day. It's a birthright. With such frequency, you get creative. In many periods of Italian history, people found their cupboards bare and took up the challenge to eat as well as possible. *La cucina povera*, the poor kitchen, means frugal cooking born of necessity. The *cucina povera* became the cornerstone of Italian cuisine and fostered a philosophy of innovation. For every *pranzo* or *cena*, lunch or dinner, a bowl of spaghetti or tagliatelle was carried to the table. In lean times, the pasta might have been graced just with slivers of *finocchiona* (salami with fennel) and oregano, or with foraged porcini and dashes of olive oil. Chestnuts, the blue flowers of borage and wild chicory, snails, almonds, field greens such as nettles, mint, truffles, and asparagus—every gift of the land will find a way to the pasta bowl. There's the bunch of chard that might wilt by tomorrow, the overabundance of basil by the back door, meaty eggplants, and bright red and yellow peppers, just waiting to hit the olive oil, garlic, and ubiquitous crunchy breadcrumbs. (Because Italians usually buy bread daily, the toasted leftover slices often become a prime topping.)

Years of cooking with Tuscans have made me an admirer of their intrinsic instinct for spontaneity. Because pasta provides the chance for countless innovations, there exist out in the ether thousands of recipes never committed to paper. Lucky accidents happen as fast as leftover sausages, or roasted vegetables, or a wedge of pecorino can journey from fridge to stove. They're devoured—then forgotten.

A few years back, my husband, Ed, announced that he wanted to try a different pasta every day of the year. We began to pay more attention to great things that *just happened* on a random Wednesday night. Instead of forgetting those last-minute inspirations, I began to write down the combination of pistachios, shallots, and chickpeas; the *sedanini* (pasta shaped like little celery stalks) with prosciutto, onion, and peas; the mini-farfalle with big garlic and toasted walnuts. I remembered how much we relished the shrimp and fennel we'd stirred into fusilli. When our neighbor Ivan mentioned that for Saturday lunch he was chopping an onion, throwing together some sausage and peas, then stirring in a little tomato at the end, I envied his family pulling up their chairs for a bowl of that quick invention. Naturally, I drove home and made it myself, which is so often how I've learned here in Tuscany. He didn't say what kind of pasta he planned to use, so I selected *gigli*, one of my favorites—a twirl of pasta that flares open at the tip like its namesake, lilies.

Susan, a frequent traveler to Italy, *Food & Wine* editor, and constant host of splendid dinner parties, had her stash of personal favorites. After the evening when her lemon pistachio inspired us, we began to gather our notes for speedy pastas that we've loved over the years and to experiment with combinations we'd never tried before. How many nights am I home late, or Ed invites someone impulsively, and pasta saves us? I wish I had time to haul out the *spianatoia,* the wooden pasta board every passionate Italian cook owns, and spend long mornings listening to Monteverdi while rolling out pasta. Those days are cherished but seldom.

No surprise: Ed and I were unable to cook 365 pastas, day by day. Life interferes. But we did amaze ourselves with how many nights we'd cut open that box of rigatoni, improvise with what we found, and *butta la pasta!* That's the cry often heard in Italian kitchens: Throw in the pasta; time to eat!

Although we treasure slow afternoons making our own agnolotti, gnocchi, or ravioli, we're more often in the kitchen at dark, ravenous and facing a fridge with a distinctly odd assortment of choices. How to triumph over that demon, time? Dried pasta. Always at hand.

In this collection of *veloce* recipes, Susan and I share our shortcuts and tips, such as cooking in a large (10- to 12-inch/25 to 30 cm) skillet on high heat like chefs. This saves minutes and locks in flavor. We make good use of food processors and blenders. They're handy, as is the small spice blender previously relegated to a bottom drawer but perfect for chopping parsley, a couple of shallots, nuts, and herbs. A potato masher saves minutes when you are browning ground meat and sausage. Hand chopping is satisfying and precise, even meditative, but electric helpers save time. In each recipe, our priority is to see how to combine steps to streamline the process. In a pinch, at the grocery store, grab fresh vegetables already sliced or chopped. Another time saver—*mise en place*. If you assemble all your tools and ingredients as you begin, you stay focused and save time. And you're not running all over the kitchen while the garlic burns.

Stocking the kitchen with goods ordered from a variety of purveyors expands choices. Having on hand dried porcini mushrooms, prosciutto, guanciale, and other cured artisan *salume*, preserved lemons, good pecorino, vacuum-packed cooked chestnuts, and many other treats gives your imagination free rein.

The most fun comes with stocking the cupboards with a variety of dried pastas. Spaghetti, linguine, fettucine, lasagna, and macaroni are known to all, but this book also celebrates the other myriad shapes that simple flour, water, and sometimes egg can become. Luckily for those outside of Italy, we

have many choices available beyond the usual. And overnight delivery makes ordering the less-known pastas simple. *Ruote* (wheels), *torchietti* (little torches), *cavatappi* (corkscrews), *paccheri* (packages), *lumache* (snails), *orecchiette* (little ears), and dozens of others— so many useful shapes add surprise and delight in the kitchen. And shouldn't that be our motto—surprise and delight? For each recipe, we suggest an appropriate pasta, but improvising is the heart of *veloce* cooking.

We're steeped in tradition, but in *Pasta Veloce*, we're also celebrating creativity. We've also been inspired by a new generation of chefs who respect their heritage but are breaking rules and moving the cuisine forward. Pesto

thickened with breadcrumbs rather than pine nuts? What about toasted almond and red pepper pesto, or green garlic? Pasta cooked in red wine? Cook the greens in the pasta? A splash of coffee or red vermouth? What works, what's quick, what lifts the spirits and attention? We schemed to discover shortcuts to classics, such as ragù, even eggplant Parmigiana. We love taking ideas from *secondi* (traditional meat courses) and adapting them to pasta because we often want pasta to be dinner, not just a first course. That's how our duck confit and chestnut recipe (page 192) evolved, also the lamb loin (page 188) and the beef filet mignon with black olives, balsamic onions, and garlic (page 184). As pasta ingredients, expensive cuts of meat stretch far—a bonus.

Most of our recipes aim to be ready in that quick time between filling the pot with water and the draining of the pasta. A few are longer but still ASAP. This gets dinner to the table pronto, or leaves more time for preparing a *secondo*, the next course, or setting a beautiful table. Speed is good.

Susan and I have cooked together in Mexico, Tuscany, Rome, Puglia, and Sicily, as well as in the United States. Since our early forays, when we both were learning our moves through Julia Child's *Mastering the Art of French Cooking*, we've been friends. In our twenties, we were serving veal Prince Orloff, cassoulet, and boeuf bourguignon to an appreciative group of friends. Susan turned food pro in New York, and I went off to writing and teaching pursuits in California. We stayed in touch through circuitous years and miraculously found ourselves, decades later, neighbors in a small North Carolina town. With ease, we took up where we had left off, with constant laden tables set for spontaneous dinners.

During the early Covid-19 pandemic, we became a "bubble." In those long months of solitude, we cooked. She lived three houses down the street. We invented pastas, either eating together or leaving a covered dish on each other's porches. What a discerning palate—I was amazed that Susan could taste that smidgen of nutmeg, or a whisper of Madeira in a sauce.

We had no guests, but we had Ed, a most appreciative taster. He kept the pasta pot boiling and the music loud. He was at the skillet, too, adding a bit more *peperoncino* (hot pepper), grating lemon zest, splashing in the vino, and making sure the pasta came out *al dente*, "to the tooth," which simply means a little firmness to the bite, not overcooked.

As poet Theodore Roethke wrote, "In a dark time the eye begins to see." The strains of forced isolation soon lifted. We were *busy*—sourcing saffron, pecorino, aged balsamic vinegar, Calabrian pancetta, and so many delightful artisan pasta types. Formerly accustomed to frequent trips to the grocery store, we found special products online that make life easy. Now we're regulars on several websites and continue to seek out quality products from elsewhere. Delivery is super quick and the choices are unlimited.

When we felt ready, we headed to my house in Tuscany, where we were joined by Steven Rothfeld, who was the photographer for *The Tuscan Sun Cookbook* and *Bringing Tuscany Home*. In *Pasta Veloce*, we agreed, we wanted to show images of our scrumptious pasta recipes and the joyous lifestyle and the place they spring from. After living for so many years at Bramasole, the abandoned villa I bought and restored so many years ago, I've never stopped marveling at the zest and exuberance of Italian life. The house seems alive on its terraced hillside of olive trees, always ready to welcome the many friends who've raised their glasses around our table. It's also alive because we keep adding pergolas, revising rooms, rethinking the garden, and meeting the demands of a three-hundred-year-old stone house with walls over a yard thick. ("Cool in summer, cool in winter," Ed reminds me.) Because of the translations of my books, people come from all over the world to take a photo of the house, sketch the garden, or leave a flower or a note. In this way, Bramasole has connected me to a wider world than I knew and has made me value *una casa aperta*, an open house, not only as a happy value but as a metaphor for how best to live.

The center of that value is the table. Throughout the book, you'll see tables set for enjoyment, as well as what will be served on each plate. You'll

see, too, people gathered in cafés, evocative shops and markets, fishermen hauling in the catch, glowing windows full of delectable pastries, and always the legendary, beneficent light of Italy.

*"A tavola!"* the Italians say. "To the table!" Candles are lit, an enticing aroma wafts from the kitchen. Held aloft, the steaming bowl of pasta arrives. We invite you to the pleasures of pasta and the vivacity of Italian life. Here you have it, *Pasta Veloce*.

# Lilies and Wheels, Shells and Shirtsleeves: The Shapely Art of Pasta

What astounding variety! Much Italian whimsy and smarts go into shaping pasta. The person who invented *radiatori* must have been cold. Otherwise, you have to wonder why someone forms a pasta in the shape of a radiator. Books have been written, and shops in Italy sell posters illustrating the myriad forms pasta takes, but no one ever has covered *all* the pencils, rings, cigarettes, spindles, knots, navels, wheels, lilies, candles, whistles, and nails that have inspired novices, home cooks, and chefs to shape the dough differently. Many inventions were spontaneous. Maybe this time the dough takes on a short, cylindrical form, like the half-sleeve (*mezze maniche*) that *nonna* is sewing on the summer shirts.

Not that shapes are arbitrary. Just that pasta shapes are a playful art, not a categorical science. Italians swear by certain pastas for particular ingredients. Spaghetti and other long ribbon and strand pastas are often selected for ragùs and hearty sauces, such as the classic spaghetti alla puttanesca—the old favorite that uses anchovies, tomatoes, capers, olives, chiles, and lots of olive oil, all waiting on the pantry shelf. But then it is paradoxical that long pastas are also preferred with some more delicate seafood recipes featuring lobster, clams, and mussels. The whole story in this case is that, overall, spaghetti rules. Ubiquitous all over Italy and the world, spaghetti is the universal donor.

Some sauces have firm traditions with a certain type of pasta; it seems just wrong to meddle with those. Imagine my Italian neighbors saying, "What's this?" if they spotted *farfalle* (butterflies) served with clams. Pasta with clams wants to pair with spaghetti, or flatter linguine. It's a law. Linguine has variations in *trenette* (ribbons) and *bavette* (little dribbles), neither of which *ever* is served with clams.

Passionate opinions range over what shape calls for what sauce. We recommend, except for a few written-in-stone combinations, to keep it flexible. In the dry pastas, basically, there are the long, the shaped or cupped, and the tubular, with many variations of each. Within the types, mix and match.

Tagliolini, angel hair, farfalle, spaghettini, all the light pastas, naturally lend themselves to delicate sauces, especially those made with spring vegetables—young peas, asparagus, green garlic pesto—or the ethereal golden caviar (page 116). It seems as if the farther south you go in Italy, the bigger the pasta and the more rustic the recipe. *Ziti, paccheri, tortiglioni, conchiglioni, quadrettoni, rigatoni*—all oversized—seem devised for the heartiest of sauces. It just makes sense that a pasta with dense eggplant and tomatoes, or a mixed seafood extravaganza, or a baked pasta with sausage needs to be substantial. Hollow pastas like *paccheri* and rigatoni hold the sauce—and hold up to the sauce. And all twisted or round forms such as shells naturally hold sauces in their cups and folds. In Tuscany, however, a mighty ragù often appears with a rather more delicate tagliatelle—and that's where we believe pasta pairing enters the zone of delight, where it's fun to cook, the zone of *do what you will*. Although a pasta shape suggests its best use, we believe that there's enormous leeway in the choice.

A pleasure of travel is the surprise of how a particular pasta belongs to a place. The thick spaghetti known as *pici* is seldom encountered outside Tuscany.

*Trofie* arose in Liguria. The small *fregola* that's almost like couscous you rarely encounter outside Sardinia. *Spaghetti alla chitarra*, as if cut by guitar strings, speaks of Abruzzo, and the black squid ink pasta, so integral to calamari and octopus, recalls the pleasures of the Venetian lagoon.

In *Pasta Veloce*, we bring the news from different regions of Italy. All the saved notes and photos of mine from Sicily, Friuli, Valle d'Aosta, and Lazio continue to inspire. Who could forget the *orecchiette*, ear-shaped pasta, with bitter greens, served on a terrace facing the vibrant piazza of Monopoli in Puglia? The simple *tajarin* pasta with butter and sage devoured under a vine-draped pergola while visiting Barolo in Piemonte? The luxurious linguine with lobster at a seafront trattoria in Alghero, Sardinia? When you're in these places, it's as if you *must* sample the intrinsic taste of where you are.

A main distinction is whether the pasta is *rigate* or *liscio*, striated or smooth. Some, such as *paccheri* and penne, come both ways. The ridges help

a light vegetable sauce or a meaty ragù to adhere. We adore our big, tubular Paccheri with Eggplant, Red Bell Peppers, Onion, and Tomatoes (page 74). The sauce speaks with a way-south Basilicata accent. Smooth or ridged doesn't matter because this hearty vegetable mixture seeps inside the *paccheri*, as well as covering the outside. Generally, if there's a choice between smooth and ridged, why not choose the *rigate*?

When selecting dried pasta, the words *trafilata al bronzo* are important. There's a difference in texture if the dough was cut by bronze dies. Spaghetti *alla chitarra* is the most famous example, cut by a wire-stringed device resembling a guitar. If you hold a regular grocery-store pasta beside one that's bronze cut, you notice a rougher, more speckled surface that makes the sauce cling. Although most artisan dried pastas are *trafilata al bronzo*, that's not to say ordinary pasta can't measure up; it's what most Italians choose every day. Bronze cut means an extra step toward the *paradiso* of heavenly pastas.

We're always astounded at the *pastasciutta* (dried pasta) choices in a normal market in Italy, especially the long shelves of tiny pastas for soups and for children's meals: *stellini* (little stars), *perline* (little pearls), *semi di melone* (melon seeds), *occhi di pernice* (pheasant eyes), and the universal *alfabeto* (alphabet). In addition to the tiny, delicate options, there are fifty or so other shapes an Italian cook expects to choose from. In *Pasta Veloce*, we focus on these handy dried pastas, suggesting both common shapes and the more specialized.

*Frances's home Bramasole in Cortona, Tuscany*

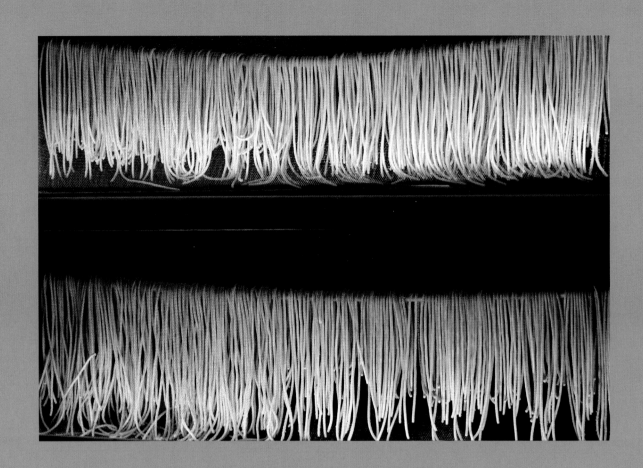

# La Dispensa della Pasta:
# The Pasta Pantry

The names of pastas provide as much fun as the shapes. While we're all familiar with standbys, we may not know the meaning of their names: spaghetti (little strings), tagliatelle (cuts), linguine (small tongues), fettucine (little cuts), farfalle (butterflies). Dozens of others delight the eye, bump up the taste, and have evocative monikers. One of the oddest names, *strozzapreti*, means "priest stranglers." Apparently, priests invited to midday Sunday *pranzo* used to be fed abundant amounts of pasta first so they wouldn't have much room for the precious meat coming next. *Strozzapreti* remains a favorite but maybe not to priests. Spaghetti comes in many sizes, from *spaghettini* (little strings) to the thick Tuscan *pici*. Discover more fun and useful shapes in the list below. Stock your kitchen with great extra-virgin olive oil, a variety of these enticing pastas, a stash of drink-me-now wines, and you're cooking like an Italian.

| | | |
|---|---|---|
| | **Bavette** | A slender ribbon pasta, slightly convex, with an imaginative name: *bava* refers to a little dribble, while *sbavare* means to full-on drool. |
| | **Bucatini** | *Buco* (hole) or *bucato* (pierced), a thicker spaghetti with a hole through it like a thin straw. |
| | **Calamarata** | Thick rings that resemble cross-sections of squid (calamari). |
| | **Capellini** | "Little hair" consists of strands that are a bit thicker than angel hair pasta. |
| | **Casarecce** | A versatile *S*-shaped twist with a name that simply means "homemade." |
| | **Cavatappi** | "Corkscrews" aptly describes the shape of this pasta. |
| | **Cavatelli** | Short, curvy hollow tubes, perfect for holding hearty sauces, especially goose and duck. The name possibly derives from *cavare*, to hollow out. |
| | **Creste di gallo** | Charmingly named after what they resemble, ruffled cocks' combs. |

| | | |
|---|---|---|
| | **Ditaloni** | Big thimbles (the larger version of *ditali*), medium-sized, and tiny *ditalini*, often used in Italian soups. All three are short tubular pastas. |
| | **Farfalle** | Shaped like butterflies. Farfalle are also called bowties. *Farfallone* are the larger ones. |
| | **Fettuccine** | Little strips, almost a twin to tagliatelle, just slightly thinner. |
| | **Foglie d'ulive** | Small and oval, shaped like olive leaves. |
| | **Fusilli** | Spindle or screw-shaped, like a part inside a rifle. Fusilli lunghi is the longer version. |
| | **Garganelli** | Inspired by a *garganel*, or chicken's esophagus. Little folded squares fold into an angular tube shape. |
| | **Gemelli** | "Twins"—but this pasta isn't two tubes twisted around each other but rather a double twist into a spiral. |
| | **Gigli** | A pretty twist-and-flare shape that evokes its namesake—lilies. |

| | | |
|---|---|---|
| | **Lumache, lumaconi, chiocciole, conchiglioni** | All snail or seashell forms, available in several sizes. The largest ones—those ending in -*oni*—are perfect with shrimp tucked inside the curves. |
| | **Maccheroni** | Now Italian slang for a blockhead, *maccheroni* originally might have meant a "meal for a funeral." This is mac and cheese pasta, though it comes in many sizes and textures. Macaroni also is a generic term for tubular pastas. |
| | **Maltagliati** | "Badly cut." These rough triangles often were hurriedly shaped from leftover bits of pasta. |
| | **Mezze maniche** | "Short sleeves," usually grooved. |
| | **Orecchiette** | "Little ears" may not sound appetizing, but the cupped shape and chewy texture make them naturals with sausage, pesto, and with bitter greens and Broccolini. |
| | **Paccheri** | "Packages," big, hollow, and mouthy tubular pasta that are designed to catch hold of the heartiest sauces. |
| | **Pappardelle** | Gulp it down, from *papparsi*, to eat greedily. These are the classic broad, flat strips used for meat sauces, especially for wild boar in Tuscany. |

| | | |
|---|---|---|
| | **Penne** | Pen-shaped tubes (quills) that come in many sizes and may be smooth (*lisce*) or ridged (*rigate*). Small penne are called *pennette*. |
| | **Pici** | The Tuscan favorite is perhaps derived from the term *appicciare*, to be sticky, though the Tuscans say not. Otherwise, the origin remains unknown. This most-favored pasta is hand rolled into long strands, thick as a knitting needle, and is available dried online. Pici is typically swathed in meat sauces but is equally good with fava beans and cherry tomatoes. |
| | **Pipe, Pipette** | Pipes, large or the diminutive size, both shaped like snails or the bowl of granddaddy's pipe. Typically they're almost pinched closed at one end. Select the *rigate* (ridged) version. |
| | **Radiatori** | "Radiators." The undulations of the radiators' ridges work well with a variety of sauces. Probably inspired by early heating, this versatile pasta should be better known. |
| | **Reginette** | "Little queens" are wide, flat ribbons with rippled edges, which are attractive to serve. Also known as *mafaldine*, it is named for the twentieth-century Italian princess of Savoy, Mafalda. Another name for reginette is *malfadine*, little Mafalda. It's sometimes more narrow. |
| | **Riccioli** | "Curly." A short hollow spiral similar to fusilli but often with a rough surface. |
| | **Rigatoni** | A big, ridged macaroni that gets its name from *riga*, line, and *rigare*, to furrow. |

| | | |
|---|---|---|
| | **Ruote** | Also called *rotelle*, resembles wheels with spokes radiating from the hubs. |
| | **Sedanini** | "Little celery stalks," a perfect pairing with light vegetable sauces. |
| | **Stracci** | "Rags." Squares are improvised from leftover dough or broken lasagna sheets. |
| | **Torchietti** | "Small torches." Use these twists like fusilli, when you want a pasta with lots of surfaces for the sauce to adhere. |
| | **Tortiglioni** | "Big twists," a cousin of rigatoni. |
| | **Trenette** | May come from Genovese dialect, *trena*, or string. Slightly thicker than other flat pastas, it's a traditional choice for pesto. |
| | **Trofie** | "Nourishment" may be the meaning of this pasta that goes back to Greek origins. The slightly thick little folds are the Ligurians' choice for their green bean and potato pasta with pesto. |

# The Transforming Ingredient: Extra-Virgin Olive Oil

*Pasta Veloce* recipes call for extra-virgin olive oil. The better the quality, the tastier the dish. Driving through the Italian countryside, you see that an ancient trinity still exists—the wheat bordered by an olive grove and a fence draped with grapevines. The wheat for pasta and bread, then the olive oil, and the wine. The eternal heart-of-hearts of local life—and still the foundation of home cooking. Excellent olive oil will transform your kitchen. I've learned to use it liberally and to count on its health properties as a bonus to Italian cooking. May we all live to one hundred!

Extra-virgin indicates that the oil is low in acid, with no more than 0.08 grams of oleic acid per 100 grams of oil. To achieve this, just-picked olives are rushed to the mill and crushed without heat or chemicals. Only this initial press results in what is called "extra-virgin." Besides incomparable flavor, fresh oil has many health benefits.

More than a decade ago, a rigorous scientific study (PREDIMED) showed that following a plant-centric Mediterranean diet over time with liberal use of extra-virgin olive oil, both raw and in cooking, resulted in a major reduction in the incidence of cardiovascular events—heart attack, stroke, cardiovascular disease—even in high-risk individuals. The study also suggested improvements in blood pressure, insulin sensitivity, cholesterol levels, inflammation, and carotid atherosclerosis. It is thought that most of these benefits result from the polyphenols (protective chemicals found in plants, which often contain valuable antioxidants). Because fresh extra-virgin is rich in polyphenols but degrades over time, it pays to search out current harvest oil from a reliable source. And use it liberally.

Lesser oils, labeled just "olive oil," "pure," or "light," do not have the opulent taste or the same health benefits. Those inferior oils are produced from the leftover pulp, called *sansa,* from the first pressing and are extracted by heat and/or chemicals, which not only affects the flavor, but destroys valuable nutrients. Sometimes you see recommendations to use your great extra-virgin olive oil for salads and vegetables only and to cook with this bland, denuded product. This is incorrect and outdated advice.

How to choose the best oil, especially with so many out there? Be knowledgeable—a lot of misinformation exists in the olive oil world. Without access to those bucolic fields and groves, how to know which olive oil to buy? Here's a primer.

*Look for information on the label that tells where the olives were harvested, *not* where the oil was bottled. You're looking for the real thing, a lively, fresh oil, not some mixture made from old and new olive oil, or something combined from several countries, possibly from different harvests or with added color.

*Check the label for the harvest date. The olives of Mediterranean countries and the United States are picked in the fall, so a 2023 harvest date will be good for all of 2024. While good oils, properly stored in a cool, dark cabinet, can be used for two years or even longer, the best taste and health benefits reside in recently pressed oil. Those diminish as time passes. Even in specialty stores, often the oil is sadly beyond its peak and even beyond the expiration date. A good producer is proud of her oil and makes sure the information on the label clearly identifies its origins, dates, and harvest information.

*"Cold pressed" is good information, even though that doesn't mean as much as it used to, since most top brands now use a modern technology that doesn't involve heat.

*Color isn't always a dependable guide. In a recently harvested oil, a bright green color usually means fresh. Tuscany is famous for its emerald green oil, but other regions, such as Greece, Spain, Liguria, and the south of Italy, produce fine oils that often are more golden in color.

*The container should be glass or metal, as plastic imparts a taste, and it's best if the glass is dark. A week on a sunny counter and oil begins to turn.

*Excellent oil is not cheap; it can't be because of the high costs of maintaining groves, paying pickers, transporting and milling the olives, then bottling and shipping the oil. At a restaurant, you might pay $20 to $30 or way more for a bottle of wine that is gone before dessert is over. A great olive oil lasts a lot longer.

When in doubt, get a recommendation from a cook or a shopkeeper you trust, and turn to knowledgeable sources, such as Nancy Harmon Jenkins's book *Virgin Territory: Exploring the World of Olive Oil* or the New York International Olive Oil Competition website (NYIOOC.org), for the best choices worldwide, plus links for ordering. I happily produce my own Bramasole Olive Oil, which consistently wins gold medals at NYIOOC and can be ordered online.

# Salt and Water: Secrets to Cooking with This Elemental Mix

For pasta, salt and water are an alchemical mix—the simple elements not only cook the pasta but also combine with the pasta's starch, which often forms part of the sauce you will serve with it.

Fill a big pasta pot about three-quarters full and bring the water to a boil. If you're cooking a smaller amount of pasta, use any saucepan with enough water for the pasta to swirl. The usual guideline is a hefty 5 to 6 quarts (4.7 to 5.7 liters) of water for a pound of pasta, but really, you just want enough water so the pasta can dance, not clump. Stir briefly as you add the pasta to the water, to allow the water to separate the pieces or strands, then give it another turn or two during cooking time.

Start the sauce when you put the pot on the burner. When the water boils, after 5 to 10 minutes, throw in the salt, which will fizz, then dissolve immediately. This is the preferred Italian way, but if you want to add the salt earlier, that's fine, too, especially if you might forget. Into the roiling salted water, add the pasta and begin timing it. With the sauce underway, by the time the pasta is done, usually 6 to 12 minutes (a few take longer), your sauce will be ready, too. Dinner in under 20 minutes is the goal, although a few of these recipes may take a bit longer.

How much salt? Some salt is saltier than others. Table salt in Italy is finer and less potent than, say, standard Morton salt. On videos, when you see Italian cooks throwing in a handful, that's why. Decide on your own the amount of salt you prefer, depending on the kind you use, the size of your pot, and your personal taste. I use a heaping 2 tablespoons. If you're adding only a teaspoon or so, the pasta will be bland. Be generous! Taste your water. Sea salt or coarse salt are preferable. Iodized salt can lend a metallic taste.

Do not add oil to pasta water—this doesn't prevent sticking, and who ever had a problem with that anyway, unless they didn't use enough water? Worse, when oil coats the pasta, sauce will not bond. For the same reason, if you rinse cooked pasta, the sauce will slide off. The clinging starch—and the pasta water—are often a necessary ingredient in creating a thickened, creamy sauce.

Check the package instructions for approximate cooking times. Often directions indicate longer cooking times than needed. Best to start checking about 2 minutes sooner than the time indicated. Most dried pastas take around 10 minutes. Thin ones—tagliatelle, spaghettini, angel hair—can be done in 4 to 6. Some, such as orecchiette, can take up to 18 minutes. Pasta is best *al dente*, to the tooth. Far south in Italy, pasta is served quite chewy. How do you like it?

Stir in the pasta without covering the pot. In some recipes, we suggest removing the pasta a minute or two before it's quite done, finishing it in the pan with the sauce so that it continues to cook while absorbing the flavors.

Before draining, retain a cup (120 ml) of pasta water should you need it for the sauce. Some pastas go directly into the sauce, lifted, still dripping, with tongs, so that the water clinging to the pasta becomes part of the sauce.

When the pasta is done, and steam rises from the pot, and the kitchen window fogs, and maybe some music is playing, there's a pleasurable moment of anticipation. The pasta is almost ready.

# Vegetables and Cheese

Artichokes are redolent of the Mediterranean sun. Travelers to Rome may find themselves ordering a different preparation at every meal—stuffed with tomatoes and breadcrumbs, fried whole, raw and thinly sliced in salads. For *veloce* pasta recipes, we rely on frozen or jarred hearts. Here, dry, salty ricotta gives a punch to the artichokes and to the other Mediterranean stars: olives and tomatoes. On most Italian tables, there is a shaker of *peperoncini*, crushed hot red peppers that add heat when you need it. The chickpeas pair with the hollow, shell-shaped pasta, giving it main-course status.

# Pipe Rigate with Artichokes, Ricotta Salata, Olives, and Tomatoes

SERVES 4 TO 6

12 ounces (340 g) pipe rigate

3 tablespoons extra-virgin olive oil

2 medium tomatoes, chopped

2 tablespoons minced oil-packed sun-dried tomatoes

2 cups (340 g) jarred or frozen artichoke hearts, thawed (see Note)

½ cup (90 g) pitted black olives, Kalamata or Gaeta

2 tablespoons lemon juice

3½ ounces (100 g) ricotta salata, cut into small dice

1 (14 ounces/380 g) can chickpeas, rinsed and drained

½ teaspoon dried thyme

½ teaspoon dried oregano

¼ teaspoon crushed hot red pepper, or more to taste

Coarse salt and freshly ground black pepper

½ cup (50 g) grated Parmigiano Reggiano

Sprigs of fresh thyme, for garnish

In a large pot of boiling salted water, cook the pasta until al dente, about 10 minutes. Scoop out and reserve ½ cup (120 ml) of the pasta water, then drain the pasta.

Meanwhile, heat the olive oil in a large skillet. Add the fresh and sun-dried tomatoes and cook over medium-high heat, stirring often, until the tomatoes soften, about 3 minutes. Add the artichokes, olives, lemon juice ricotta salata, and chickpeas. Stir well. Season with the thyme, oregano, and hot pepper, adding salt and pepper to taste. Reduce the heat to medium-low and simmer for 5 minutes.

Add the pasta to the artichoke mixture and toss to mix. Simmer for 1 to 2 minutes to heat through, adding just enough of the reserved pasta water to moisten. Serve in bowls, topped with the grated cheese. Garnish with thyme.

———

NOTE: When using frozen artichoke hearts, thaw under running cold water, pat dry, and toss in a couple of tablespoons of olive oil.

Artichokes with fennel pollen, thyme, and vivid preserved lemon conjure visions of a sun-drenched terrace shaded by a grape arbor and fig trees. Aromatic fennel pollen, available in many markets and online, is one of Italy's favorite seasonings. The honeyed anise flavor has spiced dishes of the Mediterranean world for eons. Similar to rigatoni, the tubular and deeply grooved *tortiglioni* (from *torcere*, to twist) is a marvelous pasta for intense, flavorful sauces such as this one.

# Tortiglioni with Artichokes, Herbed Onions, Tomatoes, and Lemon

SERVES 4 TO 6

12 ounces (340 g) tortiglioni

¼ cup (60 ml) extra-virgin olive oil

1 onion, finely chopped

1 teaspoon fresh oregano leaves, or ½ teaspoon dried

1 teaspoon fresh thyme leaves, or ½ teaspoon dried

¼ teaspoon fennel pollen

Coarse salt

3 medium tomatoes, coarsely chopped

1 (14½-ounce/410 g) jar marinated artichoke hearts, halved, or quartered if large, or 1 package (16 ounces/450 g) frozen artichoke hearts, thawed (see Note, page 38)

1 whole preserved lemon, chopped and seeded, or grated zest and juice of 1 lemon

¼ teaspoon crushed hot red pepper, or more to taste

½ cup (50 g) grated pecorino Romano

In a large pot of boiling salted water, cook the pasta until al dente, 10 to 11 minutes. Reserve ½ cup (120 ml) of the pasta water, then drain the pasta.

Meanwhile, heat the olive oil in a large skillet. Add the onion and sauté over medium-high heat, stirring occasionally, until softened, about 3 minutes. Season with the oregano, thyme, fennel pollen, and salt.

Add the tomatoes and cook until softened, 3 to 4 minutes. Stir in the artichokes, lemon, and hot pepper. Reduce the heat to medium and simmer for 2 minutes longer.

With tongs, add the al dente pasta directly to the skillet and toss to mix. Gradually add just enough of the reserved pasta water to moisten, probably no more than ¼ cup (60 ml). Combine well. Serve in a large bowl, topped with the cheese.

This pasta comes together so quickly that you won't even have time to finish a glass of wine while cooking! Abundant oregano and bright lemon flavor add a summertime note. Large jars of fire-roasted red peppers are handy to keep in the fridge. While we love this with *strozzapreti*, the evocatively named "priest-strangler" pasta (see page 21), *casarecce*, or penne are other good choices.

# Strozzapreti with Mozzarella, Tomatoes, Artichokes, and Mediterranean Herbs

SERVES 4 TO 6

In a large pot of boiling salted water, cook the pasta until al dente, 10 to 11 minutes. Note: ½ cup (120 ml) of the pasta water will be used while starting the sauce. At the end of cooking time, reserve 1 more cup (240 ml) of water before draining.

Meanwhile, in a large skillet, heat the olive oil over high heat until almost smoking. Add the tomatoes and cook, stirring occasionally, until blistered, about 1 minute. Add the garlic and oregano and mix well with the tomatoes. Reduce the heat to medium-high.

Toss in the artichokes and red pepper strips. Add the lemon juice and season with salt and pepper. Scoop out ½ cup (120 ml) from the boiling pasta water and add it to the artichokes. Stir in the mozzarella, reduce the heat to low, and cover the skillet. Cook until the cheese is softened, about 2 minutes.

Add the cooked pasta to the skillet along with ½ cup (120 ml) pasta water. Toss to mix, adding more pasta water if needed. Serve on plates, with the grated cheese sprinkled on top and curls of zest for garnish.

12 ounces (340 g) strozzapreti

3 tablespoons extra-virgin olive oil

12 cherry tomatoes, halved

3 cloves garlic, crushed through a garlic press

2 teaspoons fresh oregano, or 1 teaspoon dried

2 (14-ounce/400 g) cans artichoke hearts, drained

½ cup (45 g) roasted red pepper strips, drained

Juice of 1 lemon (about 3 tablespoons) plus curly strips of zest, for garnish

Coarse salt and freshly ground black pepper

4 ounces (115 g) fresh mozzarella, diced (about 1 cup)

Grated Parmigiano Reggiano or Grana Padano

This luxurious pasta can serve as the perfect main course at a springtime lunch or as a starter before almost any meal, especially chicken or fish. The extra-creamy sauce comes from the mascarpone, which adds a sweet and silky texture. This is best when asparagus comes into season and tastes like spring, but the brief roasting boosts flavor any time of year. If chives are not on hand, substitute a couple tablespoons of chopped parsley or scallion greens or a tablespoon of minced fresh tarragon.

# Farfalle with Roasted Asparagus, Lemon Cream, and Chives

SERVES 4 TO 6

Preheat the oven to 425°F (220°C). In a large pot of boiling salted water, cook the pasta until just al dente, 9 to 10 minutes. Scoop out and reserve ⅓ cup (80 ml) of the pasta water before draining.

Meanwhile, toss the asparagus with the olive oil in a bowl. Spread it out in a single layer on a large baking sheet. Roast until just tender but still bright green, 3 to 4 minutes.

In the same bowl, whisk together the egg yolk, mascarpone, ⅓ cup (35 g) of the Parmigiano, the lemon zest, salt, and pepper. Gradually whisk in the reserved pasta water.

Scrape the sauce into the pasta pot. Add back the cooked pasta and toss over medium-low heat until the sauce thickens, about 2 minutes. Do not overcook, or the egg may curdle.

Add the roasted asparagus, lemon juice, and 2 tablespoons of the chives; toss to mix. Serve with the remaining Parmigiano and chives sprinkled on top.

8 ounces (225 g) farfalle

1 large bunch asparagus (1 to 1¼ pounds/450 to 560 g), tough ends removed, stalks cut on an angle into 1-inch (2.5 cm) pieces

2 tablespoons extra-virgin olive oil

1 egg yolk

1 cup (4 ounces/115 g) mascarpone, at room temperature

½ cup (50 g) grated Parmigiano Reggiano

Grated zest of 1 lemon, plus 1 tablespoon lemon juice

½ teaspoon coarse salt

¼ teaspoon freshly ground black pepper

3 tablespoons minced fresh chives

As beautiful as it is appealing, this colorful vegetarian pasta is something of a conversation piece. Susan prefers to serve the beets on top of the pasta and let guests mix them in as they like. Cream cheese is common in Italian shops; it's called by its American producer's name, "Filla Delfia." Many markets sell time-saving, vacuum-packed cooked beets in the produce department.

# Farfalle with Beets in Goat Cheese Sauce

SERVES 4

8 ounces (225 g) farfalle

8 ounces (225 g) cooked beets, diced

1 teaspoon balsamic vinegar

1 small shallot, finely chopped

2 tablespoons extra-virgin olive oil

1 cup (240 ml) chicken broth or bouillon

4 ounces (80 g) fresh white goat cheese (see Note)

2 ounces (55 g) cream cheese

Coarse salt and freshly ground black pepper

3 tablespoons chopped fresh dill

In a large pot of boiling salted water, cook the farfalle until al dente, 9 to 10 minutes; drain the pasta.

Meanwhile, in a small bowl, toss the diced beets with the balsamic vinegar; set aside.

In a large skillet, cook the shallot in the olive oil over medium heat until softened, about 2 minutes. Pour in the broth. Add the goat cheese and cream cheese and warm, stirring, until the cheese dissolves and the sauce is creamy and smooth. Season with salt and pepper to taste. Remove from the heat.

Add the hot cooked pasta to the sauce and toss to coat evenly. Divide among four shallow bowls or plates and distribute the beets among them. Top with the chopped dill.

———

NOTE: If your market sells 4-ounce (115 g) packages of fresh white goat cheese rolled in herbs, use that. It will add even more flavor.

Called rapini in Italy, broccoli rabe in America, this winter vegetable is actually not a form of broccoli at all, even though it looks like a lushly overgrown Broccolini. Instead, it's a close cousin to the turnip, which perhaps accounts for its slight bitterness that many find appealing. The entire vegetable— flower, leaves, and stalk—is edible, though the thicker end of the stem can be a bit tough and are best trimmed off. The Puglian favorite, pasta *orecchiette*, is another good choice for this recipe.

# Penne Rigate with Spicy Broccoli Rabe and Toasted Garlic

SERVES 4 TO 6

In a large pot of boiling salted water, cook the penne rigate until al dente, 10 to 11 minutes. Scoop out and reserve 1 cup (240 ml) of the pasta water, then drain the pasta.

Meanwhile, in a large deep skillet, heat 3 tablespoons of the olive oil. Add the garlic and cook over medium-high heat until the garlic just begins to darken, about 2 minutes. Stir in the anchovy paste and hot pepper and cook until the garlic is lightly toasted, about 1 minute longer; do not brown. Quickly pour in ⅓ cup (80 ml) plain water to stop the cooking.

Add the broccoli rabe to the pan and toss to coat with the flavored oil. Cover and cook, stirring occasionally, until it is just tender but still green, about 3 minutes.

Add the cooked pasta along with ½ cup (120 ml) of the reserved pasta water. Toss to mix. Simmer for 1 to 2 minutes to heat through, adding more cooking water if needed to moisten. Drizzle on the lemon juice and the remaining 1 tablespoon olive oil and add salt to taste. Serve with a generous sprinkling of grated cheese.

12 ounces (340 g) penne rigate

¼ cup (60 ml) extra-virgin olive oil

4 large cloves garlic, sliced

1 teaspoon anchovy paste

½ to 1 teaspoon crushed hot red pepper

1 large bunch broccoli rabe (about 1 pound/450 g), tough stem ends removed, remainder cut into 1½- to 2-inch (4 to 5 cm) pieces

1 tablespoon fresh lemon juice

Coarse salt

Grated pecorino Romano or Parmigiano Reggiano

In waste-not Italy, broccoli stalks are peeled, cut into chunks, and steamed with the florets. Time consuming for our purposes, but try this if you have time. One of the healthiest of the cruciferous vegetables, broccoli has potent cancer-fighting chemicals that do best when lightly cooked, as here. To save time, purchase a prepared bag of broccoli florets.

# Casarecce with Broccoli, Garlic, and Shaved Pecorino

SERVES 4 TO 6

Bring a large pot of salted water to a boil. Add the broccoli and cook for 2 minutes, or until bright green and crisp-tender. Use a sieve to remove the broccoli; rinse briefly under cold running water to stop the cooking; set aside.

Add the pasta to the same boiling water and cook until al dente, 10 to 11 minutes. Scoop out and reserve 1 cup (240 ml) of the pasta water, then drain the pasta.

Meanwhile, in a large skillet, cook the garlic in the olive oil over medium heat until softened and fragrant, about 2 minutes. Stir in the anchovy paste, if using, and hot pepper; remove from the heat.

As soon as the pasta is ready, add it to the skillet along with the cooked broccoli. Toss to mix, adding the reserved pasta water as needed to moisten. Season with salt and black pepper. Transfer to a large serving bowl and toss with the shaved pecorino.

12 ounces (340 g) broccoli, separated into florets (about 5 cups)

8 ounces (225 g) casarecce

3 cloves garlic, thinly sliced

3 tablespoons extra-virgin olive oil

½ teaspoon anchovy paste (optional)

¼ teaspoon crushed hot red pepper

Coarse salt and freshly ground black pepper

1½ ounces (40 g) pecorino Romano, in one chunk, thinly shaved with a vegetable peeler

**Florets of chartreuse Romano,** sometimes called "broccoli Romanesco," resemble little forest trees in a fairy tale. The whorls branch out in a spiraling Fibonacci pattern, making it fascinating to look at. A relative of broccoli and cauliflower, broccoli Romano tastes like a combination of both. The sauce adheres well to the *cavatelli* (corkscrews). Regular broccoli will work as well, if the Romano is out of season.

# Cavatelli with Broccoli Romano in Creamy Parmigiano Sauce

SERVES 4 TO 6

8 ounces (225 g) cavatelli

1 onion, chopped

3 cloves garlic, slivered

¼ cup (60 ml) extra-virgin olive oil

Coarse salt and freshly ground black pepper

1 head broccoli Romano (about 12 ounces/340 g), divided into florets

1 cup (240 ml) heavy cream

2 tablespoons fresh lemon juice, plus strips of zest for garnish

¾ cup (75 g) grated pecorino Romano

In a large pot of boiling salted water, cook the pasta until al dente, 9 to 10 minutes. Scoop out and reserve ½ cup (120 ml) of the pasta water, then drain the pasta.

Meanwhile, in a large skillet, sauté the onion and garlic in the olive oil over medium-high heat until the onion is softened and translucent, 3 to 4 minutes.

Steam the broccoli Romano until it is tender enough for a fork to pierce it with a little resistance, 4 to 5 minutes. Reserve a handful of florets for garnishing the plates.

In a food processor, combine the remaining florets with the sautéed onion and garlic. Add the cream and lemon juice. Puree until smooth, adding as much of the reserved pasta water as needed to create a thick, creamy sauce.

Scrape the sauce back into the skillet, add the drained pasta, and toss to coat. Reheat over medium heat, tossing, until hot. Divide among bowls or plates. Top with the reserved florets, lemon zest, and a generous sprinkling of pecorino.

*Torchietti*, little torches, is worth the trouble of ordering online, if it is not readily available near you, because the twisted shape with flared ends holds its own so well with big sauces. Check the pasta several times, as this sturdy shape sometimes needs more time than most. *Gigli* (lilies), or even penne, is a good substitute. Paired with cabbage, beans, and creamy Fontina cheese, this is a sustaining main-course pasta. Pop open a big red to enjoy with it.

# Torchietti with Cabbage, Cannellini Beans, Onion, and Sage

SERVES 4 TO 6

In a large pot of boiling salted water, cook the pasta until al dente, 11 to 12 minutes, then drain the pasta, reserving ½ cup (120 ml) of pasta water.

Meanwhile, in a large skillet, sauté the onion in the olive oil over medium-high heat, stirring occasionally, until softened, about 3 minutes. Reserving some slivers for garnish, add the sage, allowing it to hit the oil and fry briefly.

Add the reserved pasta water to the skillet. Add the cabbage. Cover and cook until it softens, 4 to 5 minutes. Add the pureed beans, season with salt and pepper, and toss well. Reduce the heat to low and simmer for 3 to 4 minutes. Add the pasta, mix, and simmer for about 1 minute longer to warm through.

Serve in a large bowl, topped with the cheese and garnished with the remaining sage slivers.

12 ounces (340 g) torchietti

1 onion, chopped

¼ cup (60 ml) extra-virgin olive oil

12 fresh sage leaves, slivered

½ medium head Savoy cabbage (about 1½ pounds/680 g), cored and chopped

1 (15½-ounce/440 g) can cannellini beans, pureed in a food processor with the liquid from the can

Coarse salt and freshly ground black pepper

½ cup (55 g) shredded Fontina cheese

Aromatic fennel seeds plus the mild anise flavor of fresh fennel provide an herbal, pleasingly floral note to this dish. For best taste, let the onion take on a bit of color. This is a flavor-packed vegetarian pasta that doesn't even need any cheese, which makes it a great vegan option. Regular red onions work, but if you find the oblong, shiny red Tropea onions, even better. A treasure of the Calabrian table, these onions are a bit sweeter than regular red onions.

# Mezze Maniche with Cauliflower, Fennel, and Red Onion

SERVES 4 TO 6

8 ounces (225 g) mezze maniche

¼ cup (60 ml) extra-virgin olive oil

1 teaspoon fennel seeds

¼ teaspoon crushed hot red pepper

1 medium red onion, thinly sliced

½ teaspoon coarse salt

1 cup thinly sliced fresh fennel (about 3 ounces/ 90 g)

½ medium head cauliflower, separated into small florets (about 3 cups/405 g)

Chopped flat-leaf parsley and fennel fronds, for garnish

In a large pot of boiling salted water, cook the pasta until al dente, 12 to 14 minutes. Do not drain.

Meanwhile, in a large heavy skillet, heat the olive oil over high heat. Add the fennel seeds and hot pepper and cook for 30 seconds. Add the onion and salt. Sauté for 1 to 2 minutes, until the onion softens. Add the fresh fennel and continue to cook, stirring occasionally, until the fennel is softened and the onion starts to color, about 5 minutes.

Push the onion and fennel to the side of the pan, add the cauliflower, and continue to cook over high heat, stirring once, for 2 minutes, then toss with the onion and fennel. Ladle 1 cup (240 ml) of water from the pasta into the pan and continue cooking until the cauliflower is tender but still holds its shape, 5 to 7 minutes. If the vegetables become dry, add a bit more pasta water.

As soon as the pasta is al dente, ladle another ½ cup (120 ml) of the cooking water over the vegetables. Then drain the pasta, add to the skillet, and toss to mix with the vegetables. Simmer, stirring and scraping up any browned bits from the bottom of the pan, for 1 to 2 minutes. Serve garnished with a sprinkling of chopped parsley and fennel fronds.

Instead of our typical white variety, cauliflower is often displayed at Italian markets in mounds of purple and orange. Whatever the color, the slightly nutty and earthy vegetable adapts to a range of preparations. Buy a fresh head or florets already divided and packaged or finely chopped into "rice." This saves a lot of time, but you can pulse florets in your food processor to achieve the same result.

# Gigli with Riced Cauliflower, Toasted Pine Nuts, and Golden Raisins

SERVES 4 TO 6

10 ounces (280 g) gigli

1 red onion, coarsely chopped

3 tablespoons extra-virgin olive oil

1 clove garlic, minced

3 tablespoons pine nuts, or ¼ cup (35 g) finely chopped walnuts

½ teaspoon anchovy paste

¼ teaspoon crushed hot red pepper

10 ounces (280 g) riced cauliflower

1½ cups (375 ml) chicken stock or bouillon

¼ cup (40 g) golden raisins

1 tablespoon balsamic vinegar

2 or 3 scallions, thinly sliced

Grated Parmigiano Reggiano

In a large pot of boiling salted water, cook the pasta until al dente, about 10 minutes. Drain, then transfer to a large serving bowl.

Meanwhile, in a large skillet, sauté the onion in the olive oil over medium-high heat until it is softened and just beginning to color, 3 to 4 minutes. Add the garlic, nuts, anchovy paste, and hot pepper. Sauté until the nuts are lightly toasted, 2 to 3 minutes.

Add the riced cauliflower to the skillet and stir to coat with the flavored oil. Pour in the chicken stock and add the raisins and balsamic vinegar. Bring to a boil, reduce the heat to medium, and simmer until the cauliflower is just tender, about 3 minutes. Stir in the scallions.

Scrape the cauliflower sauce over the gigli in the serving bowl. Toss to coat the pasta with the sauce. Sprinkle a few tablespoons of cheese on top and pass more at the table.

Whipping up an incredibly tasty sauce with just two ingredients—cheese and a whopping amount of pepper, blended with pasta water—makes *cacio e pepe* something of a miracle. The alchemy occurs via extra-starchy water and a generous amount of just-ground black pepper. Toasting the pepper in a skillet is Ed's twist on the classic recipe. Watch it spike the flavors. Taste before adding any extra salt to the dish, since the pasta absorbs the briny cooking water and the pecorino adds salt, too.

# Spaghetti Cacio e Pepe

SERVES 4 TO 6

To ensure the cooking water is starchy enough to emulsify the sauce, bring only 4 quarts (3.8 liters) water to a boil, less than we would ordinarily use. Salt the water well and add the pasta. Cook until the spaghetti is not quite al dente, about 9 minutes. Do not drain.

Meanwhile, in a large skillet over medium heat, toast the pepper briefly, about 2 minutes. Ladle in ¾ cup (180 ml) of the pasta water that has been cooking for 3 to 4 minutes.

When the pasta is barely al dente, use tongs to transfer it to the pepper sauce in the skillet. Ladle in an additional 1½ cups (360 ml) of the pasta water. Simmer, tossing, until the water is mostly evaporated. Then add another ½ cup (120 ml) of the cooking water and toss with the pasta. As the water evaporates, add another ½ cup (120 ml) of the pasta water. Cook over medium-high heat, tossing, until most of the liquid is absorbed but the sauce remains creamy, about 6 minutes. Season with salt to taste.

In a small bowl, mix the cheese with a final ¾ cup (180 ml) pasta water to form a thick sauce. Stir into the pasta and serve immediately.

12 ounces (340 g) spaghetti

1 tablespoon coarsely ground black pepper

Coarse salt

2 cups (200 g) grated pecorino Romano

Classic carbonara, the story goes, was invented in a trattoria in Rome when American soldiers after World War II longed for the bacon and eggs of home. Silky and unctuous, the sauce of egg yolks and cheese clings to the pasta, and the pancetta adds a robust zap of flavor. Since salt is in the pancetta, the cheese, and the pasta water, taste before adding any more. Guanciale cut into short strips, or bacon, can be substituted for the pancetta. If using those, drain away most of the fat after they're cooked.

# Linguine alla Carbonara

SERVES 4 TO 6

In a large pot of boiling salted water, cook the pasta until al dente, 10 to 11 minutes. Do not drain.

Meanwhile, in a large skillet, cook the pancetta in the olive oil over medium-high heat, stirring occasionally, until it is golden but not crisp, 4 to 5 minutes. Remove from the heat.

While the pancetta cooks, whisk the egg yolks well in a medium bowl, then mix in the Parmigiano and 2 tablespoons plain water.

When the pasta is al dente, use tongs to transfer it directly to the skillet. Add ¼ cup (60 ml) of the pasta water and toss over medium-high heat to mix the pasta with the pancetta and oil. Add a few turns of the pepper mill. Add salt to taste. Remove from the heat.

Gradually whisk another ¼ cup (60 ml) of the pasta water into the egg yolks and cheese, then pour the mixture over the pasta in the skillet. Toss to coat well. Serve at once, topped with the pecorino Romano.

12 ounces (340 g) spaghetti

3 tablespoons extra-virgin olive oil

5 ounces (140 g) pancetta, cut into small dice

5 egg yolks

½ cup (50 g) grated Parmigiano Reggiano

¼ cup (25 g) grated pecorino Romano

Freshly ground black pepper and coarse salt

Fettuccine Alfredo is another of those alchemical creations where something sublime results from simple ingredients. Originally from Rome, the dish was made with just butter—lots of butter—and finely grated Parmigiano Reggiano emulsified into a creamy sauce with the starchy pasta water. Because our butter does not have the amount of fat the Italian version has, this process becomes tricky. To prevent the cheese from clumping, a bit of reduced heavy cream creates a glossy and luxurious sauce. Grate the cheese in the food processor, running it long enough to produce a fine texture. The unusual amount of salt in the pasta water is because the amount of water is reduced in this recipe.

# Fettuccine Alfredo

SERVES 4

1 tablespoon coarse salt

10 ounces (280 g) fettuccine

⅔ cup (160 ml) heavy cream

⅛ teaspoon freshly grated nutmeg

⅛ teaspoon freshly ground black pepper

5 tablespoons (2½ ounces/70 g) unsalted European-style or Irish butter, such as Kerrygold, diced (see Note)

1 cup (100 g) finely grated Parmigiano Reggiano

Additional salt and black pepper to taste

In a large saucepan, bring 3½ quarts (3.3 L) water to a boil. Add the salt and fettuccine and cook, stirring occasionally, until the pasta is al dente, 12 to 14 minutes. Use less water than usual because the starch in the cooking water is a major ingredient in the sauce.

Meanwhile, in a large nonstick skillet over high heat, bring the cream to a boil. Add the nutmeg and pepper. Boil for 2 minutes, stirring, then reduce the heat to very low and simmer for 3 minutes, or until the cream is thickened and reduced by about half. Add the butter and let it partially melt.

When the pasta is ready, use tongs to transfer the fettuccine to the skillet. Add ½ cup of the pasta water and toss over low heat. Sprinkle on ¾ cup (180 ml) of the cheese and toss until the pasta is nicely coated with the thick, creamy sauce. Season with additional salt and pepper to taste.

Divide among four plates or shallow bowls and sprinkle 1 tablespoon of the remaining cheese on top of each serving.

———

NOTE: Most domestic butters contain 14 percent butterfat. Widely available Irish butter has 15 percent, and "European-style" butter, if made in the United States, tops out at 16 percent. The higher the butterfat, the more stable the emulsion will be.

Home late again? Too busy to cook? Hungry after school? Or at midnight? *Fonduta*, creamy melted cheese sauce, the ultimate comfort food, could not be simpler. This recipe is only a "for instance," as there are endless ways to vary fonduta. Taleggio, Parmigiano, Fontina, Montasio, and even Gruyère are all excellent cheese choices. Also use leftover bits of cheese melted together. Here, this ultimate comfort food is paired with broccoli. Other Italian variations just as tempting include:

- Black or white truffle shaved over the top
- Chopped escarole, cooked briefly in the prepared fonduta
- Crispy pancetta (or bacon), crumbled over the sauce
- Slivers of prosciutto or slices of cooked sausage, stirred in
- Sautéed garlic and chopped walnuts
- Zucchini cubes sautéed in extra-virgin olive oil and mint
- Asparagus cut in pieces, steamed al dente
- Sautéed thinly sliced mushrooms

# Spaghetti with Fonduta and Broccoli

SERVES 4 TO 6

In a large pot of boiling salted water, cook the pasta until al dente, 9 to 10 minutes. Do not drain.

Meanwhile, in a medium saucepan, steam the broccoli until barely fork-tender, 3 to 4 minutes. Drain the water and toss the florets with the olive oil. Season with salt and pepper. Set aside.

In a large skillet, melt the butter over low heat. Pour in the cream and add the Taleggio. Simmer, stirring until the cheese melts, about 2 minutes. Season with salt and pepper.

When the pasta is al dente, use tongs to transfer it directly into the fonduta with the water clinging to the strands. Mix well, then toss with the broccoli and Parmigiano. Serve at once.

12 ounces (340 g) spaghetti

1 pound (455 g) broccoli florets, each sliced 3–4 times

2 tablespoons extra-virgin olive oil

Coarse salt and freshly ground black pepper

4 tablespoons (55 g/ ½ stick) unsalted butter

⅔ cup (160 ml) heavy cream

4 ounces (115 g) Taleggio cheese, cut into small cubes

¼ cup (25 g) grated Parmigiano Reggiano

A subtler and more complex mac and cheese, this baked pasta is scrumptious on its own, but really sings with a drizzle of intense Ten-Minute Tomato Sauce (page 62). Use traditional elbow macaroni, if you like, instead of the *gigli*. This is a pasta dish that does well prepared in advance and baked off shortly before serving, if that's more convenient. Italian provolone has a more pronounced flavor than the domestic.

# Baked Gigli with Four Cheeses and Ten-Minute Tomato Sauce

SERVES 4 TO 6

8 ounces (225 g) gigli

3½ ounces (135 g) imported or aged provolone, coarsely grated (about 1½ cups)

1 cup (8 ounces/250 g) whole-milk ricotta

½ cup (50 g) grated Parmigiano Reggiano

¾ teaspoon coarse salt

½ teaspoon coarsely ground black pepper

¼ teaspoon freshly grated nutmeg

6 ounces (170 g) fresh mozzarella, diced (about 1½ cups)

½ cup (15 g) lightly packed flat-leaf parsley

½ medium shallot, sliced

⅔ cup (80 g) panko

¼ teaspoon crushed hot red pepper

2 tablespoons extra-virgin olive oil

Ten-Minute Tomato Sauce (optional; recipe on page 62)

Preheat the oven to 450°F (230°C). In a large pot of boiling salted water, cook the pasta until just al dente, 9 to 10 minutes. Scoop out ½ cup (120 ml) of the pasta water, then drain the pasta.

Meanwhile, in a mixing bowl, combine the provolone, ricotta, Parmigiano, ½ teaspoon of the salt, the black pepper, and the nutmeg. Blend well. Stir in the reserved pasta water and fold in the mozzarella. Turn into an oiled 14-inch (36 cm) oval gratin or other shallow flameproof baking dish.

In a food processor, pulse the parsley and shallot to chop coarsely. Add the panko, hot pepper, and remaining ¼ teaspoon salt. Whirl to combine. Sprinkle the seasoned breadcrumbs over the pasta and drizzle the olive oil on top.

Bake until heated through, 7 to 8 minutes. Turn the heat to broil and broil for about 2 minutes, until the pasta is bubbling and the crumb topping is browned. Serve as is, or with a drizzle of tomato sauce, if desired.

# TEN-MINUTE TOMATO SAUCE

MAKES ABOUT 1¾ CUPS (420 ML)

3 tablespoons extra-virgin olive oil

2 cloves garlic, finely chopped

½ teaspoon crushed hot red pepper

2 tablespoons tomato paste

Pinch sugar

⅓ cup (80 ml) dry white wine

1 teaspoon dried marjoram, or ½ teaspoon dried oregano and ½ teaspoon dried thyme

½ teaspoon coarse salt, plus more to taste

1½ cups (about 14 ounces/410 ml) canned chopped tomatoes with their juices

2 tablespoons slivered fresh basil

In a large deep skillet, heat the olive oil. Add the garlic and sauté over medium-high heat for about 1 minute, until fragrant, without letting it brown. Add the hot pepper and sauté for 30 seconds longer. Add the tomato paste and sugar and cook, stirring, until it darkens, about 2 minutes.

Pour in the white wine and add the marjoram and salt. Boil over high heat for 1 minute to reduce. Add the tomatoes, reduce the heat to medium, and cook the sauce at a slow boil—it will splatter; partially cover, if necessary—for 5 to 7 minutes, to develop the flavors. Stir in about ½ cup (120 ml) water to adjust the thickness. Add the basil and season with additional salt to taste.

Our version of this surprising high-low combination of extravagant and humble ingredients is inspired by a favorite of mine on the menu at La Loggetta, which was featured in a scene of the movie *Under the Tuscan Sun* and is now a popular restaurant in the arcaded medieval fish market. Overlooking the main piazza in Cortona, an outside table is a fine perch for people watching as well as for tasting regional specialties. This recipe's origin harks back to *la cucina povera*, the poor kitchen. Cabbage, a staple of frugal cooking, combines with highly prized truffles, which are widely available to woodcutters and farmers who find them on their land. Locals still have their secret spots for truffles, porcini, and other wild mushrooms. For those who do not forage, they're worth a splurge when the aromatic tubers are in season. Tagliolini is simply a thinner tagliatelli. Or use spaghettini if you like.

# Tagliolini with Cabbage and Black Truffles

SERVES 4 TO 6

In a large pot of boiling salted water, cook the pasta until al dente, 7 to 9 minutes. Do not drain.

Meanwhile, in a large skillet, toss the cabbage with the olive oil over medium-high heat. Season with ½ teaspoon salt and several good turns of the pepper mill. Stir in the wine and ¼ cup (60 ml) of the pasta water. Cover the skillet and cook until the cabbage is just tender, about 5 minutes. Reduce the heat to low and stir in the cheese.

When the pasta is done, transfer it with tongs directly into the skillet. Toss to mix well, adding a little more pasta water if needed to moisten. Divide among individual pasta bowls and shave the truffles on top.

12 ounces (340 g) tagliolini

½ medium head Savoy cabbage (about 1½ pounds/680 g), cored and shredded

3 tablespoons extra-virgin olive oil

Coarse salt and freshly ground black pepper

¼ cup (60 ml) dry white wine

¾ cup (75 g) grated Parmigiano Reggiano

½ to 1 ounce (14 to 28 g) black truffles

Red bell peppers and chickpeas provide substantial texture in this dish, and along with the black olives, a range of colors—red, black, and gold—scattered with vivid green herbs. We're using canned chickpeas in this recipe. In our *orto* (vegetable garden), we've found that *ceci* (chickpeas) grow easily. Their sage-green foliage puts forth sweet pink and white flowers that even look pretty in a perennial bed. Harvesting them connects you to an ancient agricultural practice. When the bushes appear dry in early summer, we take them out to a hillside on a windy day and rub the branches and pods together. The wind takes away the skins, leaving the *ceci*. A small penne or fusilli is a good substitute if you don't have *sedanini* (little celery stalks) on hand.

# Sedanini with Chickpeas, Red Bell Pepper, and Olives

SERVES 4 TO 6

In a large pot of boiling salted water, cook the pasta until al dente, 10 to 11 minutes. Do not drain.

Meanwhile, in a large skillet, sauté the onion in the olive oil over medium-high heat, stirring occasionally, until softened, about 3 minutes. Add the bell pepper and continue to cook until the pepper is almost fork-tender but still retains a little bite, 2 to 3 minutes longer. Toss in the chickpeas, then add the olives, thyme, rosemary, salt, and black pepper.

When the pasta is al dente, use a sieve to transfer it directly to the skillet. Toss well with the bell pepper and chickpeas, adding a little of the pasta water, if needed, for moisture. Mix in half the parsley.

Transfer to a large serving bowl and garnish with the rest of the parsley. Pass the cheese separately.

———

NOTE: Olives and the oil they yield are an intrinsic part of Italian culinary heritage. Of the more than five hundred varieties that are produced, two of the most widely enjoyed black olives are Gaeta and Taggiasca. Here in the United States, our choices are more limited, so Kalamatas, of Greek origin, are offered as a substitute; they are especially convenient for *veloce* recipes because they are sold already pitted. The others are easily available online.

12 ounces (340 g) sedanini

1 onion, chopped

¼ cup (60 ml) extra-virgin olive oil

1 large red bell pepper, cut into long slivers

1 (15½-ounce/450 g) can chickpeas, rinsed and drained

½ cup (60 g) pitted and sliced Kalamata or Gaeta olives (see Note)

1 tablespoon fresh thyme, or 1½ teaspoons dried

1 teaspoon minced fresh rosemary

Coarse salt and freshly ground black pepper

Handful fresh flat-leaf parsley, chopped

Grated Parmigiano Reggiano

**Pea shoots are delicate** yet full of flavor. Carrots add color and bite. Rather than turn the dish sweet, the small amount of sugar greatly enhances the natural taste of both the pea shoots and carrots. This is a nice lunch for children, slipping in the vegetables with the pasta. For grown-ups, this performs as a subtle prelude to just about any *secondo*.

# Spaghettini with Charred Carrots and Pea Shoots

SERVES 4

8 ounces (225 g) spaghettini

¼ cup (60 ml) extra-virgin olive oil

8 ounces (225 g) carrots (about 2 large), peeled and coarsely shredded

1 large shallot, thinly sliced

3 tablespoons unsalted butter

4 to 5 ounces (110 to 140 g) pea shoots or tendrils, cut into 2-inch (5 cm) lengths

1 teaspoon coarse salt

1 teaspoon sugar

Freshly ground black pepper

In a large pot of boiling salted water, cook the spaghettini until just barely al dente, about 6 minutes.

Meanwhile, heat the olive oil in a large nonstick skillet. Toss together the shredded carrots and shallot slices. Throw into the pan, spread out slightly, and sear over medium-high heat for 2 to 3 minutes without stirring. Some of the carrots and shallots will caramelize a bit. Add the butter, reduce the heat to medium-low, and stir until it melts.

With tongs, transfer the pasta to the skillet. Add the pea shoots. Season with the salt, sugar, and a generous grind of black pepper. Toss to mix and serve at once.

**Fist-sized aglione, elephant garlic,** tastes milder than common garlic. Antonello, electrician as well as a maestro in the kitchen, revealed his secret to enhancing this classic recipe: Reserve 2 tablespoons of the garlic and add it raw at the end, dividing the cloves and smashing them with the flat side of a knife. Also try this recipe with the more pungent regular garlic, using half as much. And add just 1 tablespoon of the raw garlic at the end. Pici is also an excellent pasta choice. Quick tip: Seasoned breadsticks make handy breadcrumbs. Just slice or roughly chop.

# Spaghetti with Elephant Garlic and Herbed Breadcrumbs

SERVES 4 TO 6

In a large pot of boiling salted water, cook the spaghetti until al dente, 9 to 10 minutes. Scoop out and reserve ½ cup (120 ml) of the pasta water, then drain the pasta.

Meanwhile, in a large skillet, heat 2 tablespoons of the olive oil. Stir in the breadcrumbs. Toast over medium-high heat, stirring often, until crisp and lightly browned, 3 to 4 minutes. Season with the oregano, thyme, ½ teaspoon salt, and ⅛ teaspoon black pepper. Set aside on a plate and wipe out the skillet.

In the same skillet, heat the other 2 tablespoons olive oil. Add all but 2 tablespoons of the garlic and cook over medium heat, stirring, until the garlic is golden and softened but not brown, 2 to 3 minutes. Pour in the wine and bring to a boil, then immediately reduce the heat to low. Season with the hot pepper.

Add the cooked pasta to the pan, along with the raw garlic. Add ⅓ cup (80 ml) of the pasta water, blending the mixture well. Add more liquid if desired but no more than ½ cup (120 ml) in total. Toss in the toasted breadcrumbs and the cheese, season with additional salt and pepper if needed, and serve at once.

12 ounces (340 g) spaghetti

4 tablespoons (60 ml) extra-virgin olive oil

1 cup (100 g) coarse fresh breadcrumbs

1 teaspoon fresh oregano leaves, or ½ teaspoon dried

1 teaspoon fresh thyme leaves, or ½ teaspoon dried

Coarse salt and freshly ground black pepper

1 cup (135 g) elephant garlic cloves, minced in a food processor or mini processor

¼ cup (60 ml) dry white wine

¼ teaspoon crushed hot red pepper

½ cup (50 g) grated Parmigiano Reggiano

This may not look like the eggplant Parm you know, but tossing pasta into the vegetables transforms it into a main course while adding another layer of taste—and in quicker time. For a more formal presentation, take a look at the variation of creating individual lasagnas suggested on page 70. Canned chopped tomatoes are pantry staples, as are Tetra Pak boxes, such as Pomi, which are imported from Italy and contain only tomatoes, no salt, acid, or other additives. The two can be used interchangeably. Outdoors on a summer evening in Rome, the plump eggplants of the Lazio region often star on the menu. Cooking at home for a group of friends, you can depend on this Eggplant Parmigiana to please everyone.

# Penne Rigate with Eggplant Parmigiana

SERVES 4

In a large pot of boiling salted water, cook the penne until just al dente, 11 to 12 minutes. Scoop out and reserve 1 cup (120 ml) of the pasta water, then drain the pasta.

Meanwhile, make the eggplant sauce. Chop the onion in a food processor; remove to a plate. In the same processor bowl, coarsely chop the eggplant cubes, pulsing 12 to 14 times.

In a large skillet, sauté the chopped onion in 3 tablespoons of the olive oil with the salt and sugar over medium-high heat, stirring occasionally, until softened and beginning to turn golden around the edges, about 3 minutes. Add the garlic and hot pepper and cook for 1 to 2 minutes longer, until the garlic is fragrant.

Add the chopped eggplant to the onion along with the remaining 2 tablespoons olive oil and the oregano. Raise the heat to high and continue to cook, stirring and scraping the bottom of the pan often, until the eggplant is soft and partially browned, 4 to 5 minutes. Stir in the tomato paste and chopped tomatoes with their liquid. Bring to a boil, reduce the heat, and simmer for 2 minutes. Season with additional salt and black pepper to taste.

Pour the eggplant sauce over the pasta and toss to mix, incorporating as much of the reserved pasta water as needed to coat nicely. Add the mozzarella and grated Parmigiano and toss lightly. Serve drizzled with a little more olive oil and pass extra cheese at the table.

10 ounces (280 g) penne rigate

1 onion, quartered

1 pound (450 g) eggplant, peeled and cut into 1-inch (2.5 cm) cubes

5 tablespoons (75 ml) extra-virgin olive oil, plus more for drizzling

½ teaspoon salt

¼ teaspoon sugar

2 cloves garlic, chopped

½ teaspoon crushed hot red pepper

1 teaspoon dried oregano

1 tablespoon tomato paste

2 cups (about 14½ ounces/410 g) chopped canned tomatoes

Freshly ground black pepper

8 ounces (225 g) shredded mozzarella or diced fresh mozzarella (about 2 cups)

⅓ cup (35 g) grated Parmigiano Reggiano

While we're used to digging into a big pan of baked pasta, these elegant individual servings are charming. There's something delightful about having your own individual lasagna. Constructed from the same ingredients as the Penne Rigate with Eggplant Parmigiana (page 69), these single-serving versions layer the eggplant sauce and cheeses with sheets of pasta cut into squares, rather than tossed all together. While "no-boil" pasta is used, the sheets are boiled briefly to make them more delicate because the baking time is so brief. This is the only recipe in the book that calls for adding oil to the pasta water. That's because the no-boil sheets have a strong tendency to stick together.

# Individual Eggplant Parmigiana Lasagne

SERVES 4

1 recipe Eggplant Sauce (page 69)

10 no-boil lasagna sheets

Extra-virgin olive oil, as needed

⅓ cup (35 g) grated Parmigiano Reggiano

8 ounces (225 g) shredded mozzarella (about 2 cups)

Sprigs fresh basil (optional), for garnish

Make the eggplant sauce per the recipe on page 69; just omit the pasta. This can be done up to a day ahead.

In a large saucepan of boiling salted water with a splash of oil, cook the lasagna sheets until they are silky tender but still hold their shape, 4 to 5 minutes. (You might want to cook a couple of extras in case there are any tears.) Drain the pasta and immediately dunk them into a bowl of cold water to make sure they don't cling together. Carefully separate any that stick.

Cut each rectangle of pasta crosswise in half. On a lightly oiled baking tray, place 4 pieces in a single layer. Cover each with about 2½ tablespoons of the eggplant sauce. Use a small offset spatula or the back of a spoon to spread evenly. Sprinkle 1 teaspoon each of the grated Parmigiano and shredded mozzarella over the eggplant sauce. Repeat 2 more times so there are 3 layers of pasta and 3 layers of filling. Top with the remaining pasta. Dust with a bit more Parmigiano and mozzarella and drizzle a little olive oil over all. The lasagnas can be assembled up to 3 hours ahead and set aside, covered, at room temperature. If you refrigerate for longer storage, remove an hour or two before baking.

Shortly before serving, preheat the oven to 425°F (220°C). Bake the lasagnas for 5 minutes, or until the cheese is melted and they are heated through. Garnish with fresh basil, if desired.

**Here's a quick version** of the classic pasta of Catania, Sicily. Who was Norma? Most probably the recipe honors the heroine of Vincenzo Bellini's opera of the same name. It's still popular in the handsome and lively city of Catania, where raucous outdoor vegetable and fish markets are major fun, and the main piazza's dignified volcano-ash-colored buildings with a whimsical elephant statue make you want to linger over a strong Sicilian coffee. Look for a firm, shiny eggplant, preferably with a dot rather than a line at the bottom. This indicates a male fruit and usually has fewer seeds. A medium macaroni or ziti are also good choices for Norma. For maximum pleasure while making this pasta, play the stupendous Maria Callas singing *Norma*.

# Mezze Maniche alla Norma

SERVES 3 TO 4

In a large pot of boiling salted water, cook the pasta until al dente, 10 to 12 minutes. Scoop out and reserve ½ cup (120 ml) of the pasta water, then drain the pasta.

Meanwhile, in a large wok or heavy skillet, heat ¼ cup (60 ml) of the olive oil over high heat. When almost smoking, add the eggplant and sprinkle with ½ teaspoon of the salt. Spread out so that as much of the vegetable as possible is in contact with the pan. Sauté, stirring occasionally to allow the surfaces to brown, until the eggplant is tender and lightly browned, 4 to 5 minutes. Remove to a bowl.

Add the remaining tablespoon olive oil to the pan. Add the garlic and sauté over medium-high heat for 1 minute to soften. Add the hot pepper and anchovy paste and cook for another minute, or until the garlic is just beginning to color.

Pour in the passata, currants, and remaining ¼ teaspoon salt. Cook over medium-high heat, stirring to caramelize the sauce slightly, 3 to 5 minutes. Reduce the heat to low, add the cooked pasta, reserved pasta water, eggplant, ricotta salata, basil, and cherry tomatoes. Toss to mix well.

———

**NOTE:** For the eggplant to cook quickly but retain some of the color and texture of the peel, remove alternating strips with a swivel-bladed vegetable peeler, leaving half of the skin intact.

8 ounces (225 g) mezze maniche

¼ cup (60 ml) plus 1 tablespoon extra-virgin olive oil

1 medium-size eggplant (about 1 pound/450 g), trimmed, half-peeled (see Note), and cut into ⅜-inch (1 cm) cubes

¾ teaspoon coarse salt

2 cloves garlic, chopped

½ to 1 teaspoon crushed hot red pepper

½ teaspoon anchovy paste

¾ cup (240 ml) passata or pureed tomatoes, diluted with ¼ cup (60 ml) water

3 tablespoons (85 g) dried currants

3 ounces (60 g) ricotta salata, cut into small dice (about ¾ cup)

2 tablespoons torn fresh basil

12 cherry tomatoes, cut in half if large

In the southern region of Basilicata in Italy, you find a trove of vigorous, flavorful pasta dishes made for big appetites. This wilder side of Italy is quickly becoming a destination, especially the town of Matera, where for centuries people lived in caves carved out of the hillside. Some of these are now boutique hotels. Don't be confused by the similar name, but Maratea is a perched seaside village on the other side of Basilicata, where you find pebbly beaches and clear waters. When a version of this was served on a balmy night at Hotel Villa Cheta, only the big moon over the sea caused as much awe.

# Paccheri with Eggplant, Tomatoes, and Red Bell Pepper

SERVES 4 TO 6

12 ounces (340 g) paccheri

¼ cup (60 ml) extra-virgin olive oil

1 onion, finely chopped

4 cloves garlic, chopped

½ red bell pepper, slivered

1 large eggplant (about 1½ pounds/680 g), finely diced

1 (14-ounce/400 g) can chopped tomatoes

2 teaspoons chopped fresh rosemary

¼ teaspoon crushed hot red pepper

½ teaspoon coarse salt

¼ teaspoon freshly ground black pepper

¾ cup (75 g) grated pecorino Romano

In a large pot of boiling salted water, cook the pasta until it is al dente, about 10 minutes; drain.

Meanwhile, into a large skillet, add the olive oil and sauté the onion over medium-high heat, stirring occasionally, until softened but not browned, about 3 minutes. Add the garlic, bell pepper, and eggplant. Cook, tossing and scraping the bottom of the pan, for about 5 minutes, until the eggplant softens.

Add the tomatoes and reduce the heat to medium. Season with the rosemary, hot pepper, salt, and black pepper. Cover and simmer for another 5 minutes. Stir in about half of the cheese.

Transfer the pasta to a large serving bowl. Mix with half the sauce, then top the pasta with the rest and the remaining cheese.

A cross between a soup and a vegetable stew, pasta fagioli is immensely satisfying, especially on a foggy winter day. The cooking time of this one-pot dish might look a little longer than other recipes in the book, but on the plus side, there's no waiting for a big pot of pasta water to boil. The *fagioli* (beans) and everything else cook together.

# Pronto Pasta Fagioli

SERVES 4

In a heavy soup pot, heat the olive oil. Add the pancetta and cook over medium heat until it exudes its fat but is not brown, about 3 minutes. Add the chopped garlic and hot pepper and cook for about 30 seconds, until the garlic is fragrant.

Add the onion, carrots, and celery, raise the heat to high, and sauté, stirring occasionally, until the vegetables are softened, 4 to 5 minutes. Add 3 cups (720 ml) of the chicken broth and 2 cups (480 ml) water and bring to a boil. Add the ditalini, bay leaf, and marjoram. Season with salt and black pepper. Boil over high heat, partially covered, until the ditalini is barely al dente, about 9 minutes.

Add the tomatoes, beans, and crushed garlic. Reduce the heat to medium and simmer for 2 minutes longer. Remove the bay leaf. If you have time, let the pasta fagioli rest for about 5 minutes before serving; the flavors will develop.

————

NOTE: To speed prep time, cut the onion, carrots, and celery into chunks and chop by pulsing in a food processor.

¼ cup (60 ml) extra-virgin olive oil

2 ounces (56 g) diced pancetta

3 cloves garlic (2 chopped, 1 crushed through a press)

½ teaspoon crushed hot red pepper

1 onion, chopped (see Note)

2 carrots, peeled and diced

2 celery stalks, strings removed, diced

4 cups (960 ml) chicken broth

1 cup ditalini (4 ounces/ 110 g)

1 bay leaf

1 teaspoon dried marjoram

Coarse salt and freshly ground black pepper

2 cups (475 ml) chopped canned tomatoes

1 (15-ounce/435 g) can white beans, drained but not rinsed

Potatoes and pasta may sound like an odd combination, but this recipe is a Ligurian classic—and a marvelous vegetarian dish. Originally it was made with tiny new potatoes cooked right along with the pasta and tossed with basil pesto. We boost the flavor by cooking sliced potatoes right along with the browned onions, then tossing them together with the pasta and green beans. Choose the thinnest green beans you can find, young beans from the farmer's market, or haricots verts. If they are thicker than you'd like, cut them in half on a diagonal. If trofie is unavailable, substitute *casarecce*.

# Trofie with Green Beans, Potatoes, and Browned Onions

SERVES 4 TO 6

8 ounces (225 g) thin green beans

8 ounces (225 g) trofie

¼ cup (60 ml) extra-virgin olive oil

8 ounces (225 g) sliced onion (2 cups)

8 ounces (225 g) small red or gold potatoes, peeled and thinly sliced

Coarse salt and freshly ground black pepper

Basil Pesto (page 200; optional)

Bring 2 pots of salted water to a boil—1 large and 1 medium. Add the green beans to the smaller pot and cook until tender but still vivid green, 3 to 4 minutes. Drain into a large colander and rinse briefly under cold running water. At the same time, add the pasta to the large pot and cook until al dente, 10 to 12 minutes. Scoop out and reserve 1½ cups (360 ml) of the pasta water. Then drain the pasta right over the green beans in the colander.

Meanwhile, heat the olive oil in a large skillet. Add the onion and sauté over high heat, stirring often, until just softened, about 2 minutes. Add the potato slices and continue to cook over high heat, stirring and turning often, until the onions are browned and the potatoes are slightly colored, 5 to 6 minutes longer. Ladle 1 cup (240 ml) of the pasta water into the skillet. Cover, reduce the heat to medium, and cook until the potatoes are tender, 3 to 4 minutes.

Add the cooked pasta and green beans to the skillet and toss to mix with the potatoes and browned onions, adding more of the reserved cooking liquid if needed to moisten. Season with salt and pepper. Serve with a drizzle of basil pesto, if using.

Fresh lemon and Parmigiano Reggiano are a match made in, well, the Italian kitchen. Blend these into a shallot-cream sauce, along with pistachios and chives, and the result is an absolutely riveting dish. Because it's so rich, it is best served as a first course. To save time and effort, chop the pistachios and parsley together by pulsing them in a food processor or a mini processor.

# Lemon Pistachio Linguine

SERVES 4 TO 6

In a large pot of boiling salted water, cook the linguine until just al dente, about 10 minutes. Do not drain.

Meanwhile, in a large heavy skillet, cook the shallots in the olive oil over medium heat until soft but not browned, 2 to 3 minutes. Pour in the vermouth and boil for 1 minute. Add the heavy cream, salt, black pepper, nutmeg, cayenne, and lemon zest. Reduce the heat to medium-low and simmer for about 5 minutes to thicken slightly.

Add the butter to the cream sauce, stirring until melted. Reserve a couple of tablespoons of chopped pistachios and parsley for garnish. Add the remainder to the sauce along with the lemon juice and chives.

When the linguine is done, use tongs to transfer it to the sauce along with any water clinging to the strands. Add ½ cup (50 g) of the Parmigiano and about ⅓ cup (80 ml) of the pasta water and toss to coat evenly. Divide among shallow pasta bowls and sprinkle a little of the reserved pistachio-parsley mixture and the remaining cheese on top.

12 ounces (340 g) linguine

2 medium or 1 large shallot, minced

2 tablespoons extra-virgin olive oil

⅓ cup (80 ml) dry vermouth or dry white wine

¾ cup (180 ml) heavy cream

½ teaspoon sea salt

¼ teaspoon coarsely crushed black pepper

⅛ teaspoon freshly grated nutmeg

Dash cayenne pepper

Finely grated zest and juice of 1 lemon (about 3 tablespoons juice)

3 tablespoons unsalted butter, cut into 4 pieces

2 ounces (55 g) shelled pistachios, finely chopped (about ½ cup)

⅓ cup (15 g) chopped fresh flat-leaf parsley

2 tablespoons minced fresh chives

⅔ cup (70 g) grated Parmigiano Reggiano

Our photographer, Steven Rothfeld, shared this surprising recipe, and his pasta sings of wild rosemary and and terraced lemon groves at Cinque Terre, the five towns of staggering beauty above the Ligurian Sea. What surprising pungency and contrast the ground fresh rosemary adds. A crisp, chilled white wine, a salad of little lettuces . . . we're there. Because you are using the outside of the fruit, select unwaxed organic lemons and limes.

# Bucatini with Lemon, Lime, and Rosemary Dust

SERVES 4 TO 6

10 ounces (280 g) bucatini

2 tablespoons fresh rosemary leaves

Finely grated zest and juice of 1 lemon (about 3 tablespoons juice

3 to 4 tablespoons lime juice, plus grated zest of 1 large lime

⅓ cup (80 ml) extra-virgin olive oil

½ teaspoon coarse salt, or more to taste

¼ teaspoon freshly ground black pepper, or more to taste

¾ cup (75 g) grated Parmigiano Reggiano

In a large pot of boiling salted water, cook the pasta until barely al dente, 8 to 9 minutes. Do not drain.

Pulverize the rosemary and the two zests in a mini-processor or blender.

Warm the olive oil in a large skillet over medium-low heat. Add the citrus zest, reserving a little for garnish, and the rosemary mixture, salt, and pepper. When the rosemary begins to sizzle, remove the pan from the heat.

When the pasta is barely al dente, transfer it with tongs directly into the skillet over medium heat. Toss to coat the pasta with the flavored oil. Reduce the heat to low and add the lemon and lime juices, then toss in half the cheese. Season with additional salt and pepper to taste. Garnish with citrus zest. Pass the rest of the cheese separately.

Inspired by the popular restaurant classic butternut squash ravioli, flavored with Parmigiano cheese and a hint of sweet almond from amaretti cookies, this elegant recipe contains all the same ingredients—but is assembled in a *veloce* fashion. While you could just toss everything together, for an attractive presentation, twirl nests of the cooked pappardelle with tongs onto the bottom of a platter, dollop the butternut mixture onto each circle, and then garnish with the crisp prosciutto and sage.

# Pappardelle with Butternut Squash, Prosciutto, Amaretti, and Sage

SERVES 4

In a large pot of boiling salted water, cook the pasta until al dente, 4 to 5 minutes; drain.

Meanwhile, in a large skillet, heat 2 tablespoons of the olive oil. Add the chopped celery and onion and sauté over medium-high heat, stirring often, until soft and slightly golden, 3 to 4 minutes. Add the butter and grated squash. Continue to cook, stirring often, until the squash is soft and browning in spots, about 5 minutes longer.

Stir in the amaretti, minced sage, balsamic vinegar, nutmeg, and ⅓ cup (35 g) of the grated Parmigiano. Add as much of the broth as needed to make a moist but not soupy mixture. Season with salt and pepper to taste.

In a medium skillet, cook the prosciutto in the remaining 2 tablespoons oil over medium heat until it is just crispy, about 2 minutes. Remove with a slotted spoon. Add the slivered sage to the oil and cook until crisp, about 1 minute.

To serve, arrange the pappardelle in a shallow serving dish. Dollop the butternut mixture over the pasta. Scatter the crisped prosciutto and sage with all its oil on top. Sprinkle with the remaining cheese.

------

NOTE: For quicker preparation, chop the celery and onion together in a food processor. Then, in the same processor bowl, grate the chunks of peeled squash. Many supermarkets sell butternut squash already peeled and cut up.

8 ounces (225 g) pappardelle

¼ cup (60 ml) extra-virgin olive oil

1 celery stalk, finely chopped (see Note)

1 small onion, finely chopped

2 tablespoons unsalted butter

1¼ pounds (565 g) peeled and chunked butternut squash (5 to 6 cups), shredded in a food processor

4 amaretti cookies, mashed into coarse crumbs (a scant ¼ cup/25 g)

2 teaspoons minced fresh sage, plus 2 additional tablespoons shredded

1 teaspoon balsamic vinegar

¼ teaspoon freshly grated nutmeg

½ cup (50 g) grated Parmigiano Reggiano

1 cup (240 ml) chicken or vegetable broth

Coarse salt and freshly ground black pepper

2 ounces (55 g) sliced prosciutto, cut into thin strips

Blending cheese, salty olives, and savory sun-dried tomatoes, rich with umami, all spiked with garlic, fragrant rosemary, and a generous amount of cracked black pepper, produces a richly flavorful pasta sauce. The combination of goat cheese and mild cream cheese makes this recipe feel both rich and light. Because the olives and sun-dried tomatoes as well as the pasta water are all salty, no extra salt is added to the sauce.

# Malfadine with Goat Cheese, Olives, and Sun-Dried Tomatoes

SERVES 4 TO 5

8 ounces (225 g) malfadine

4 ounces (115 g) fresh white goat cheese, at room temperature

4 ounces (115 g) cream cheese, at room temperature

2 teaspoons chopped fresh rosemary

2 cloves garlic, chopped

1 teaspoon coarsely cracked black pepper

⅓ cup (80 ml) extra-virgin olive oil

⅔ cup (80 g) pitted black Kalamata olives, halved

⅓ cup (40 g) oil-packed sun-dried tomatoes

In a large pot of boiling salted water, cook the pasta until al dente, 10 to 12 minutes. Scoop out and reserve 1 cup (240 ml) of the pasta water; drain the pasta.

Meanwhile, in a food processor, combine the goat cheese, cream cheese, rosemary, garlic, and pepper. Whirl until well blended. With the machine on, drizzle in the olive oil through the feed tube. Add the olives and sun-dried tomatoes and pulse until chopped.

Return the pasta to the pot you cooked it in along with ½ cup (120 ml) of the reserved pasta water. Add the goat cheese mixture and toss over medium heat until just warmed through, adding as much of the remaining cooking water as needed to coat the pasta.

Pretty and light as its name, this butterfly pasta starts off a summer dinner on a colorful note: Do you cut the stem end off cherry tomatoes? At our table one night in Florence, a chef friend stared at his pasta and said he'd never return to the restaurant because the stem end was not removed. "Lax," he said. *Harsh*, we thought. But we have ever since removed the offending little spot.

# Farfalle with Basil Pesto, Ricotta, Yellow Peppers, and Cherry Tomatoes

SERVES 4 TO 6

12 ounces (340 g) farfalle

¼ cup (60 ml) extra-virgin olive oil

1 pound (450 g) cherry tomatoes, halved

1 large yellow bell pepper, slivered

3 cloves garlic, minced

12 ounces (340 g) whole-milk ricotta

½ cup (120 ml) Basil Pesto (page 200)

Coarse salt and freshly ground black pepper

Basil leaves, for garnish

In a large pot of salted water, cook the pasta until al dente, 9 to 11 minutes.

In a large skillet, heat the oil and add the tomatoes. Turn the heat to high and roll them around to blister for a minute. Add the bell pepper and lower the heat to medium, stirring until the pepper softens, about 3 minutes. Add the garlic and toss for another minute.

Add the ricotta in spoonfuls, followed by the pesto. Lightly mix with the vegetables. Season with salt and several good grinds of pepper.

When the pasta is al dente, scoop it out of the water with a sieve directly into the sauce. Toss to mix. Garnish the plates with basil leaves.

Either sweet or dry marsala will work here, though the sweet offers more intense flavor. Both impart a sweetness that balances the slightly acidic flavor of the tomato-based sauce. Baby bellas are called for, but almost any mushroom, such as white button or maitake, can be used.

# Spaghettini with Chunky Mushrooms in Marsala Tomato Sauce

SERVES 4 TO 5

In a large pot of boiling salted water, cook the spaghettini until just barely al dente, 7 to 8 minutes. Scoop out and reserve 1 cup (240 ml) of the pasta water, then drain.

Meanwhile, in a large deep skillet, melt the butter in the olive oil over high heat. Add the mushrooms and shallot and sauté, tossing, until the mushrooms are lightly browned and beginning to give up their juices, 3 to 5 minutes. Season with the salt and black pepper.

Pour in the Marsala and boil until reduced by half. Add the chopped tomatoes, chicken broth, marjoram, and hot pepper. Reduce the heat to medium and boil slowly for 5 minutes to reduce slightly.

Add the spaghettini along with ½ cup (120 ml) of the reserved pasta water. Simmer, tossing, until the pasta is al dente and has absorbed enough sauce to thicken, adding more reserved water, if needed.

12 ounces (340 g) spaghettini

3 tablespoons unsalted butter

2 tablespoons extra-virgin olive oil

12 ounces (340 g) baby bella (cremini) mushrooms, trimmed and quartered

1 medium shallot, thinly sliced

½ teaspoon coarse salt

¼ teaspoon freshly ground black pepper

¼ cup (60 ml) Marsala or Madeira

1 (28-ounce/800 g) can chopped tomatoes

¾ cup (175 ml) chicken broth

1 teaspoon dried marjoram

Pinch of crushed hot red pepper

Susan had a party for her book *Cooking for a Crowd* at the original Union Square Café in New York City, with recipes from the book. They liked the Three Mushroom Lasagna with Gorgonzola Cream Sauce so much, they kept it on the menu for six months. Here is a quicker presentation, which skips the layering of lasagna, and instead simply spreads the mushroom filling over pasta and drizzles the sauce. Best served as a first course, this could be the star of a very special meal. The ripple-edged reginette is perfect but any of the flat-strand pastas, such as linguine and tagliatelle, work well, too.

# Reginette with a Trio of Mushrooms in Gorgonzola Cream Sauce

SERVES 6

12 ounces (340 g) reginette

3 tablespoons extra-virgin olive oil

¼ ounce (7 g) dried porcini mushrooms, coarsely chopped (about ½ cup)

8 ounces (225 g) baby bella (cremini) mushrooms, halved or quartered

1 large shallot, coarsely chopped

3 tablespoons unsalted butter

3½ to 4 ounces (100 to 115 g) shiitake mushrooms, stemmed and sliced

2 teaspoons fresh lemon juice

½ teaspoon dried tarragon

Coarse salt and freshly ground black pepper

Gorgonzola Cream Sauce (page 90)

Grated Parmigiano Reggiano

In a large pot of boiling salted water, cook the pasta until al dente, 10 to 12 minutes. Drain and toss with 1 tablespoon of the olive oil to prevent sticking.

Meanwhile, in a heatproof bowl, cover the porcini with 1½ cups (360 ml) boiling water. Let stand to soften while you prepare the other mushrooms. Combine the baby bella mushrooms and shallot in a food processor and pulse about a dozen times, until the shallot is finely chopped and the mushrooms are minced.

In a large heavy skillet, melt the butter in the remaining 2 tablespoons olive oil. Add the mushroom and shallot mixture and sauté over high heat, stirring occasionally, until the mushrooms start to brown, 5 to 7 minutes. Add the sliced shiitakes and season with the lemon juice, tarragon, and salt and pepper. Sauté 1 minute longer. While the mushrooms are cooking, make the Gorgonzola cream sauce.

With a small fine strainer, scoop the porcini out of their soaking water and add to the skillet. Pour in 1 cup (240 ml) of the porcini soaking water and simmer for a couple of minutes to impart the flavor. Stir two-thirds of the Gorgonzola sauce into the mushrooms.

To serve, arrange the cooked pasta on a platter. Spread the mushroom filling over the pasta and drizzle the remaining sauce on top. Pass a bowl of grated Parmigiano on the side.

# GORGONZOLA CREAM SAUCE

MAKES ABOUT 2 CUPS (480 ML)

2 tablespoons unsalted
butter

2 tablespoons all-purpose
flour

1 cup (240 ml) light cream
or half-and-half

⅛ teaspoon cayenne pepper

¼ teaspoon freshly grated
nutmeg

5 ounces (140 g)
Gorgonzola dolcelatte

½ cup (50 g) grated
Parmigiano Reggiano

Coarse salt

In a small heavy saucepan, melt the butter over medium heat. Add the flour and cook, stirring, for 1 to 2 minutes without allowing the flour to color. Whisk in the cream. Bring to a boil, and keep whisking until smooth. Season with the cayenne, and nutmeg. Reduce the heat to low; add the Gorgonzola and simmer, stirring, until melted. Stir in the Parmigiano and season with salt to taste.

Use any mushroom or a mix. This makes a great first course when roasted chicken or meat follows. We like the irregularly shaped maltagliata, but a flat pasta such as linguine or tagliatelle also works.

# Maltagliata with Mushrooms, Truffle Oil, Shallots, Parsley, and Cream

SERVES 4 TO 6

In a large pot of boiling salted water, cook the pasta until al dente. Reserve ½ cup (120 ml) of the pasta water.

Meanwhile, in a medium skillet over medium heat, add the olive oil and sauté the shallots and garlic for 3 minutes, scooting them around the pan so they don't brown. Add the mushrooms, season with salt and pepper, and raise the heat to high. Continue stirring until the mushrooms slightly give to the tines of a fork, about 4 minutes.

In a small bowl, mix the reserved pasta water and the cream. Pour this into the mushrooms and heat slightly while you stir. When ready to serve, stir in the truffle oil and parsley.

Divide the pasta among bowls and top with the cheese.

------

**NOTE:** Truffle-flavored oil is a finishing oil that should be drizzled on or stirred in just before serving. Cooking it will destroy the flavor. Because of its pungency, it is best used sparingly. Like good extra-virgin olive oil, truffle oil is not inexpensive. Lesser products are made artificially—and bits of truffle in the bottle do not ensure quality. Look for a respected brand from a company that deals in fresh truffles, such as Urbani or Sabatino, or one that is noted for quality food products, like D'Artagnan.

12 ounces (340 g) maltagliata

3 tablespoons extra-virgin olive oil

2 shallots, minced

3 cloves garlic, minced

4 cups (100 g) thinly sliced mushrooms

Coarse salt and freshly ground black pepper

½ cup (120 ml) heavy cream

1 to 2 teaspoons white truffle oil, to taste (see Note)

¾ cup (30 g) chopped fresh flat-leaf parsley

½ cup (50 g) grated Parmigiano Reggiano

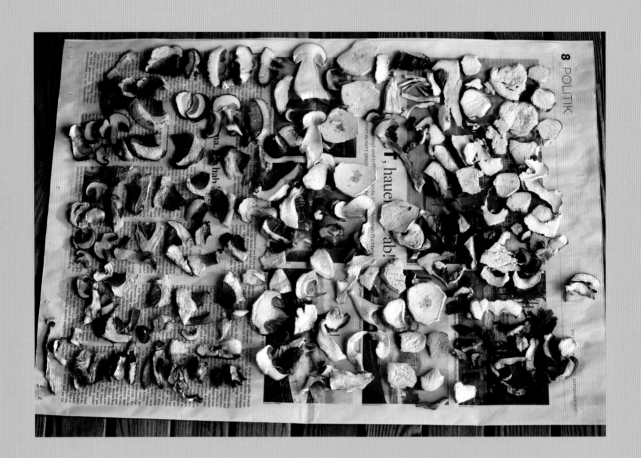

**Woodsy, crunchy—what a quick** treat, and attractive, too. Sun-dried tomatoes, too, often need a boost, especially if dry-packed and leathery. If you have those, put them in a jar when you buy them, cover with extra-virgin olive oil, and store in the fridge. Moist oil-packed tomatoes are easier to work with. A speedy tip for plumping the dried mushrooms: Crumble the porcini into a small heatproof bowl, cover with water, and microwave on high for two minutes.

# Pappardelle with Dried Porcini Mushrooms, Sun-Dried Tomatoes, and Croutons

SERVES 4 TO 6

In a large pot of boiling salted water, cook the pasta until al dente, 10 to 12 minutes. Drain the pasta.

If not microwaving the mushrooms, crumble them into a small bowl and barely cover them with hot water. Let them soak for 10 minutes.

Heat 2 tablespoons of the olive oil in a large skillet. Add the bread cubes and season with the oregano, thyme, and salt. Toast over medium heat, stirring often, until lightly browned, about 2 minutes. Remove them to a paper towel. Wipe out the skillet.

Heat the remaining 3 tablespoons (45 ml) olive oil in the same skillet. Add the onions and sauté over medium-high heat until softened and translucent, about 3 minutes. Add the sun-dried tomatoes and garlic and continue to cook for another 3 minutes.

Remove the porcini from the water. Add them to the pan, stirring to blend. Season with salt and pepper. Simmer for 2 minutes. Add ¼ cup (60 ml) of the porcini water and the cream and simmer for a minute.

Add the pasta to the sauce and toss to coat. Divide among individual pasta bowls. Top with the croutons, basil, and cheese.

12 ounces (340 g) pappardelle

1½ ounces (40 g) dried porcini mushrooms

5 tablespoons (75 ml) extra-virgin olive oil

2 slices rustic bread, cut into cubes

1 teaspoon fresh oregano, or ½ teaspoon dried

1 teaspoon fresh thyme, or ½ teaspoon dried

¼ teaspoon coarse salt, plus more as needed

1 onion, finely chopped

3 tablespoons chopped oil-packed sun-dried tomatoes

3 cloves garlic, smashed and minced

Freshly ground black pepper

½ cup (120 ml) heavy cream

5 to 6 basil leaves, torn into small pieces

½ cup (50 g) grated Parmigiano Reggiano

In Italy, this seasonal dish would be made with *friggitelli*, the small pale green peppers coveted in the summer. Shishito peppers belong to the same family, and they look identical, although smaller, which is why we use them. A trick for imbuing the peppers with a smoky taste is to get the pan fiery hot before adding them. This pasta is good warm or at room temperature, which makes it excellent for a picnic or outdoor entertaining, especially since it holds well overnight.

# Casarecce with Shishito Peppers, Anchovies, Tomatoes, and Ricotta Salata

SERVES 4 TO 6

8 ounces (225 g) casarecce

¼ cup (60 ml) extra-virgin olive oil

8 ounces (225 g) shishito peppers, stemmed

3 cloves garlic, halved lengthwise, then thinly sliced crosswise

¼ to ½ teaspoon crushed hot red pepper

16 grape tomatoes, halved (about 1½ cups/225 g)

2 ounces (55 g) ricotta salata, shaved (see Note)

2 ounces (55 g) flat anchovy fillets, drained and cut in half or thirds

¼ cup (40 g) sliced almonds, lightly toasted

Freshly ground black pepper

In a large pot of boiling salted water, cook the pasta until al dente, about 9 to 11 minutes. Scoop out and reserve ¾ cup (180 ml) of the pasta water before draining.

Meanwhile, warm a slick of olive oil in a large cast-iron or other heavy skillet over high heat. When the oil begins to smoke, add the peppers and cook, tossing occasionally, until they are softened and lightly charred, 3 to 4 minutes. Remove to a bowl.

Reduce the heat to medium. Add the remaining olive oil, the garlic, and hot pepper. Cook, stirring once or twice, until the garlic is just beginning to color, 2 to 3 minutes. Add the grape tomatoes and toss over the heat for a minute to warm them through. Return the peppers to the pan.

Add the pasta and reserved pasta water. Simmer over low heat, tossing, for 1 to 2 minutes. Remove from the heat and fold in the shaved ricotta salata, anchovies, and half the toasted almonds along with a generous grind of black pepper. Serve with the remaining almonds sprinkled on top.

————

NOTE: Ricotta salata can be shaved easily on the slicing slide of a box grater or with a cheese slicer.

For those who love a touch of bitterness, this sophisticated pasta with the counterpoint of sweet and tangy balsamic vinegar will be a favorite, especially as a first course. It's truly an instant recipe and easy to perfect if you have a large well-seasoned cast-iron skillet or griddle. Nuts, such as the walnuts here, are best when fresh, because they can go off surprisingly fast. Store them in the freezer.

# Fusilli with Grilled Radicchio, Balsamic Onions, Gorgonzola, and Walnuts

SERVES 4 TO 6

In a large pot of boiling salted water, cook the pasta until just al dente, about 10 minutes. Scoop out 1 cup (240 ml) of the water, then drain the pasta.

Meanwhile, heat a large cast-iron grill pan or skillet over high heat. Add 2 tablespoons of the olive oil, stirring in the sliced radicchio and any wayward bits. Cook for about 30 seconds. Turn with tongs and continue to cook, tossing a few times, until wilted and lightly browned, 2 to 3 minutes in all. Reduce the heat slightly if the radicchio starts to char. Remove to a plate.

In a large heavy skillet, heat 3 tablespoons of the olive oil over medium-high heat. Add the onion, sprinkle with the salt, and sauté, stirring often, until the onion is tender and lightly browned, 3 to 5 minutes. Add the balsamic vinegar, reduce the heat to medium-low, and simmer until most of the vinegar is absorbed, 1 to 2 minutes.

Stir in the honey. Add the grilled radicchio, pasta, reserved pasta water, and cheese. Toss to mix. Simmer, tossing occasionally, until most of the liquid is absorbed and the pasta is tender. Toss in the walnuts and season with salt and pepper to taste. Drizzle on the remaining 1 tablespoon olive oil and serve at once.

8 ounces (225 g) fusilli

6 tablespoons (90 ml) extra-virgin olive oil

1 head radicchio (about 10 ounces/280 g), cut into ¼-inch (6 mm) strips

1 red onion, thinly sliced

½ teaspoon coarse salt

3 tablespoons balsamic vinegar

1 tablespoon honey

4 ounces (110 g) Gorgonzola dolcelatte, diced

3 ounces (85 g) coarsely chopped walnuts (about 1 cup)

Freshly ground black pepper

Whether lunch is in the garden or at a desk, everybody loves the freshness and pungency of this summery sauce that comes together as fast as you can throw ingredients into the pan. Use a mound of any mixed herbs; substitute some peppery arugula, if you like.

# Spaghetti with Tomato Sauce and a Cup of Herbs

SERVES 4 TO 6

12 ounces (340 g) spaghetti

3 tablespoons extra-virgin olive oil

1 onion, chopped

3 cloves garlic, thinly sliced

Coarse salt and freshly ground black pepper

2 large tomatoes, chopped

1 (14½-ounce/410 g) can chopped tomatoes

1 cup (50 g) finely chopped mixed fresh herbs (parsley, thyme, rosemary, basil, oregano, chives, marjoram)

½ cup (50 g) grated Parmigiano Reggiano

In a large pot of boiling salted water, cook the spaghetti until al dente, 9 to 10 minutes.

Meanwhile, in a large skillet, heat the olive oil. Add the onion and sauté over medium-high heat, stirring occasionally, until softened, about 3 minutes. Add the garlic and continue to cook for another 1 to 2 minutes without browning.

Mix in the fresh and canned tomatoes and cook, still over medium heat, stirring, until the tomatoes soften and form a thick sauce, about 5 minutes. Stir in the herbs.

When the pasta is al dente, drain and add it to the sauce. Simmer for about a minute to warm through. Serve in bowls, with a generous sprinkling of cheese on top.

This version of the old favorite finishes cooking the pasta in the tomato sauce. What perks up the standard recipe? Taking a tip from Michelin-starred Italian chef Andrea Aprea, we use three types of tomatoes: sweet cherry tomatoes, plump Campari tomatoes, and for body, San Marzano. The result is an intense, complex flavor.

# Spaghetti al Pomodoro

SERVES 4 TO 6

In a large pot of boiling salted water, partially cook the pasta, about 6 minutes.

Meanwhile, in a large saucepan or deep skillet, heat 2 tablespoons of the olive oil over high heat. Add the whole garlic cloves and cherry tomatoes and cook, stirring only once, for 2 minutes to lightly char the tomatoes. Add the Campari tomatoes and basil sprigs. Season with the salt and the sugar. Stir in another tablespoon of the olive oil, cover, and reduce the heat to medium. Cook, stirring once or twice, until the tomatoes break down, about 4 minutes. Add the garlic and mash into a coarse sauce with the back of a large spoon or a large fork.

Now salt the boiling water and add the pasta. Cook for 6 minutes, until barely al dente.

While the pasta cooks, add the canned tomatoes and their juices to the sauce in the skillet. Cover, raise the heat to medium-high, and cook, stirring once or twice, for 5 minutes. Fish out the basil sprigs and season the sauce with additional salt to taste.

With tongs, add the partially cooked spaghetti to the sauce. Also add a ladle of the pasta water. Simmer the spaghetti in the sauce, tossing with tongs and adding another ladle or two of pasta water if needed, until the spaghetti is just al dente, about 3 minutes. Serve garnished with the slivered basil and a thin drizzle of the remaining olive oil. Pass the cheese separately.

12 ounces (340 g) spaghetti

4 tablespoons (60 ml) extra-virgin olive oil

2 cloves garlic, peeled and crushed with the side of a knife

8 to 12 cherry or grape tomatoes, cut in half

4 Campari tomatoes, cut into 6 or 8 wedges each

3 sprigs basil, plus 3 to 4 tablespoons (7.5 to 10 g) slivered fresh basil leaves for garnish

½ teaspoon coarse salt, plus more as needed

¼ to ½ teaspoon sugar

1½ cups (14 ounces) canned San Marzano tomatoes, with their liquid, cut into chunks

Grated pecorino Romano or Parmigiano Reggiano

Arrabbiata means "angry," the fiery touch that characterizes this Roman pasta. Italian shops and markets sell transparent packages of the peppery seasoning, and picking up a few to tuck into your luggage, along with pine nuts and dried porcini, is a good idea. Your clothes will be scented with aromas of Italy! Two teaspoons of hot pepper is not too much. For some, it won't be enough. Chili crisp obviously isn't an Italian ingredient, but a spoonful of this Chinese import adds a bit more heat and a tantalizing flavor.

# Pappardelle all'Arrabbiata

SERVES 4 TO 6

10 ounces (280 g) pappardelle

3 large cloves garlic, chopped

2 teaspoons crushed hot red pepper

3 tablespoons extra-virgin olive oil

¼ cup (55 g) tomato paste

½ cup (120 ml) dry white wine

1½ cups (340 g) chopped canned tomatoes

Pinch sugar

1 tablespoon chili crisp (optional)

Coarse salt and freshly ground black pepper

Shaved pecorino Romano and/or Parmigiano Reggiano

In a large pot of boiling salted water, cook the pappardelle until it is barely al dente, about 10 minutes. Do not drain.

Meanwhile, in a large deep skillet, cook the garlic and hot pepper in the olive oil over medium heat until the garlic is soft but not brown, about 2 minutes. Add the tomato paste, raise the heat to medium-high, and fry the paste, stirring until it turns darker in color and breaks up in the oil, 2 to 3 minutes longer.

Pour in the wine and boil for 1 minute. Add the chopped tomatoes and sugar. Simmer for 2 to 3 minutes to blend the flavors. Stir in the chili crisp if you are using it. Season with salt and black pepper.

When the pasta is just barely al dente, transfer it directly into the sauce with tongs. Ladle in ⅓ cup (80 ml) of the pasta water and toss well. Simmer over low heat for 1 to 2 minutes to finish cooking the pasta. Serve topped with shavings of cheese and a generous grind of black pepper.

A crowd-pleaser, this unbelievably simple pasta was hugely popular in trattorias in Italy for years before it took the United States by storm in the 1980s. No way is it dated, though. Instead, the synergy between the alcohol in the vodka and the hot pepper is very much keyed to our contemporary infatuation with spicy food. We're presenting the basic recipe here, but you can easily dress it up with frozen peas and/or strips of prosciutto, or sautéed pancetta or mushrooms.

# Penne with Vodka Sauce

SERVES 4 TO 6

In a large pot of boiling salted water, cook the pasta until just al dente, 10 to 11 minutes.

Meanwhile, in a medium saucepan, combine the vodka, hot pepper, and butter. Set over medium heat and bring to a boil; continue to cook until the butter melts, about 3 minutes. Stir in the passata and cream. Season with ¾ teaspoon salt and a generous grind of black pepper. Return to a boil.

Drain the pasta and add to the sauce. Simmer in the sauce over low heat for 2 minutes. Add the cheese and toss to mix well. Season with additional salt and pepper to taste.

12 ounces (340 g) penne

¾ cup (180 ml) vodka

1½ to 2 teaspoons crushed hot red pepper

4 tablespoons (60 g/ ½ stick) unsalted butter, cut into pieces

1½ cups (360 ml) passata

½ cup (120 ml) heavy cream

Coarse salt and freshly ground black pepper

¾ cup (75 g) grated Parmigiano Reggiano

Rich and memorable! Serve this to your best friends. All you need is a fresh truffle or two, black or white. Truffles are tricky and ephemeral but worth these quirks. Order online if they're not available in a local specialty market. Better yet, when you travel to Italy, schedule a truffle-hunting expedition in Umbria, Piemonte, Marche, or Tuscany. Truffle slicers make nice gifts but, really, a vegetable peeler works well, too. Different areas of Italy use local cheeses such as Taleggio for truffle pasta. Parmigiano is typical in Tuscany, but in Piemonte (where the white truffle reigns) robiola is popular. The amount of truffle suggested can be adjusted upward, according to budget.

# Tagliatelle with Truffles, Butter, and Cream

SERVES 4 TO 6

12 ounces (340 g) tagliatelle (see Note)

4 tablespoons (60 g/ ¼ stick) unsalted butter

¾ cup (180 ml) heavy cream

¾ cup (75 g) grated Parmigiano Reggiano

Coarse salt and freshly ground black pepper

½ to 1 ounce (14 to 28 g) fresh truffles

In a large pot of boiling salted water, cook the pasta until al dente, about 7 minutes.

Meanwhile, melt the butter in a large skillet over low heat. Stir in the cream, then add the cheese, letting it melt into the butter and cream. Season lightly with salt and pepper.

When the pasta is al dente, use tongs to transfer it directly into the skillet. Toss to coat with the sauce. Shave about three-fourths of the truffle over the pasta and mix well. Serve the pasta in individual bowls, shaving the remaining truffle over the top.

———

NOTE: If you can find fresh tagliatelle or tagliolini, which cooks very quickly, the delicacy is a good option with truffles.

For summer evenings with the grill fired up, a bowl of pasta salad fits right in. Assembling earlier in the day gives the flavors a chance to meld.

# Fusilli and Vegetable Salad

SERVES 8

In a large pot of boiling salted water, cook the fusilli until al dente, about 10 minutes, then drain.

In a large serving bowl, mix the tomatoes, yellow and green bell peppers, scallions, marjoram, mozzarella, and arugula. In a separate small bowl, whisk the olive oil and lemon juice together, then quickly whisk in the cream, salt, and pepper. Set the dressing aside.

Drain the pasta into a colander and cool it under cold water, shaking off the water and patting the pasta with a paper towel to dry it a bit.

Toss the pasta with the vegetables and add the salad dressing. Taste for seasoning. Mix well and scatter the basil on top. Serve at room temperature or refrigerate until ready to serve and toss again before serving.

1 pound (450 g) fusilli

3 large ripe tomatoes, cut in chunks

1 yellow bell pepper, cut into slivers

1 green bell pepper, cut into slivers

1 bunch scallions, thinly sliced

1 teaspoon fresh marjoram or thyme leaves

10 ounces (300 g) mozzarella, cubed

1 handful arugula, tough stems removed

½ cup (120 ml) extra-virgin olive oil

Juice of 1 lemon (about 3 tablespoons)

3 tablespoons heavy cream

½ teaspoon fine salt

½ teaspoon freshly ground black pepper

10 or so fresh basil leaves

If you have a vegetable garden, chances are that in season you're overwhelmed by zucchini, zucchini, zucchini. What often goes to waste are the blazing gold flowers that bloom without developing zucchini. These are the males. If you're lucky enough to harvest some or find them at a local farmers' market, slice a few and add them to this recipe, or other summer pastas. A couple of whole blossoms makes a beautiful garnish. Also, try baking them, each lightly filled with a spoonful of ricotta, some Parmigiano, and herbs. Drizzle olive oil over them and run them in a 350°F (180°C) oven for 20 minutes. *Ruote*, wheels, are sometimes called *rotelli*. Visually, they mimic the zucchini rounds. Penne works nicely here, too.

# Ruote with Zucchini, Tomatoes, and Shallots

SERVES 4 TO 6

12 ounces (340 g) ruote

5 tablespoons (75 ml) extra-virgin olive oil

2 large shallots, minced

4 small or 2 medium zucchini (1 pound/450g), sliced into thin coins

½ teaspoon coarse salt

3 or 4 medium yellow and/or red tomatoes, chopped

Juice of ½ lemon (about 1½ tablespoons)

4 to 5 fresh mint leaves, slivered, plus a sprig for garnish

6 to 8 zucchini blossoms, three of them slivered (optional)

½ cup (50 g) grated Parmigiano Reggiano or Grana Padano

Rosemary sprigs, for garnish

In a large pot of boiling salted water, cook the pasta until it is al dente, about 10 minutes. Scoop out 1 cup (240 ml) of the pasta water, then drain the pasta.

Meanwhile, in a large skillet, cook the shallots in the olive oil over medium heat until softened but not browned, 2 to 3 minutes. Add the zucchini and salt. Raise the heat to medium-high and sauté, stirring occasionally, for 3 minutes.

Add the tomatoes and lemon juice and continue to cook until the zucchini is tender but still firm, about 2 minutes longer.

Add the pasta to the vegetables along with ½ cup (120 ml) of the reserved pasta water. Toss gently, adding more pasta water, if needed. Fold in the mint and slivered zucchini blossoms, if using. Transfer to a serving bowl and top with the grated cheese. Garnish with a sprig of mint and rosemary and more zucchini blossoms, if using.

**Halved grape tomatoes, which** tend to remain sweet and red all year round, are a good choice for this brightly colored pasta. Top with either Parmigiano Reggiano or pecorino Romano. *Ditaloni* is an open-ended and short tubular pasta named for thimbles.

# Ditaloni with Zucchini, Tomatoes, and Peas

SERVES 4 TO 6

In a large saucepan of boiling salted water, cook the ditaloni until al dente, about 9 minutes. Reserve ½ cup (120 ml) of the pasta water, then drain.

Meanwhile, in a small bowl, toss together the tomatoes, garlic, marjoram, ½ teaspoon salt, and ¼ teaspoon pepper.

In a large skillet, sauté the zucchini in the olive oil over high heat, tossing often, until just tender but still bright green, 3 to 4 minutes. Add the tomatoes and sauté, tossing, for 1 minute, just until warmed through. Add the peas and cook for 1 minute longer.

Add the drained pasta and reserved pasta water to the vegetables in the skillet and toss to mix. Simmer, stirring gently, for 1 minute to heat through. Serve drizzled with more olive oil and a sprinkling of coarse salt.

8 ounces (225 g) ditaloni

1½ cups (300 g) diced ripe red tomatoes

2 cloves garlic, minced

1 teaspoon fresh marjoram or thyme leaves, or ½ teaspoon dried

Coarse salt and freshly ground black pepper

3 tablespoons extra-virgin olive oil, plus more for drizzling

2 cups (300 g) diced zucchini (3 small or 2 medium)

1 cup (140 g) frozen peas

# Seafood

Rich and glam, this luxurious pasta has been a party pleaser for a long time, but here is a super-quick version definitely worth a second glance. Because it's such a treat, golden caviar sets the tone for the perfect first course on New Year's Eve or any celebratory meal. Candlelight, Prosecco, and then let the toasts begin.

# Glittering Angel Hair with Golden Caviar

SERVES 4 TO 6 AS A FIRST COURSE

1 large shallot, chopped

½ cup (120 ml) heavy cream

⅓ cup (80 ml) dry vermouth

1 teaspoon coarsely cracked black pepper

1 wide strip lemon zest

1 tablespoon Cognac or brandy

Coarse salt

6 ounces (180 g) angel hair pasta

1¾ to 2 ounces (50 to 55 g) golden whitefish caviar

2 tablespoons minced fresh chives

In a small heavy saucepan, combine the shallot, cream, vermouth, black pepper, and lemon zest. Bring to a boil, reduce the heat to medium-low, and simmer until the sauce is reduced by about one-third, 4 to 5 minutes. Add the Cognac and season with salt to taste. (The sauce can be made up to 3 hours ahead; cover and set aside. Refrigerate if holding longer.)

In a large pot of boiling salted water, cook the angel hair until just al dente, 2 to 3 minutes. Meanwhile, briefly reheat the cream sauce and strain into a large serving bowl.

Drain the pasta and add to the sauce. Toss gently to coat. Add two-thirds of the caviar and chives and toss again. Using a large ladle and a long narrow fork or tongs, twirl the pasta into "nests," placing each in a shallow bowl. Top with the remaining caviar and chives and serve at once.

Pasta al *vongole* is as easy as it is delicious. At seaside trattorias all along the Italian coasts, waiters are presenting this favorite. All it takes for success is two main ingredients: fresh clams, the smaller the better for tenderness, and plenty of garlic. Cook the garlic until it is soft and beginning to color, but not browned. Also key is not overcooking the clams. A little butter added to the olive oil provides extra richness and a silkiness that helps the sauce cling to the pasta.

# Linguine with White Clam Sauce

SERVES 4 TO 6

Rinse the clams and let them soak in a large bowl of cold water for up to 30 minutes until needed.

In a large pot of boiling salted water, cook the pasta until barely al dente, 7 to 10 minutes. Reserve ½ cup (120 ml) of the pasta water before draining.

Meanwhile, in a large skillet, melt the butter in the oil over medium heat. Add the garlic and cook until soft and just beginning to color around the edges, 2 to 3 minutes. Add the marjoram, hot pepper, and salt. Set aside off the heat until the pasta is almost cooked.

When the pasta is almost ready, pour the wine into the skillet and bring to a boil over high heat. Add the clams, cover, and cook until they *just* open, 3 to 4 minutes. Watch closely because it happens fast. Discard any that do not open.

Add the cooked linguine to the skillet along with the reserved pasta water. Simmer for a minute, tossing gently with tongs. Add the parsley and serve at once.

———

**NOTE:** In general, littlenecks are about half the size of cherrystones. They yield about 15 to the pound, whereas cherrystones are closer to 10 to the pound. If using littlenecks, you'll need 45 to 50; if cherrystones, 28 to 36. Very clean, sustainably farmed littleneck clams are widely available in supermarkets. Though they need to be rinsed and briefly soaked, you need not worry about sand—they can be added straight to the sauce. The larger cherrystones should be scrubbed and soaked for 20 to 30 minutes.

3 pounds (1.36 kg) littleneck or cherrystone clams (see Note)

12 ounces (340 g) linguine

2 tablespoons unsalted butter

3 tablespoons extra-virgin olive oil

4 cloves garlic, chopped

¼ teaspoon dried marjoram

¼ teaspoon crushed hot red pepper

¼ teaspoon coarse salt

½ cup (120 ml) dry white wine or dry vermouth

3 tablespoons chopped fresh flat-leaf parsley

Chili crisp, a tantalizing blend of chiles, fermented soybeans, peanuts, garlic, and oil, is one of the most popular condiments to have captivated the current culinary market. While spicy, it's not fiery, but has a complex depth of flavor that adds zest to almost anything it touches (see also page 102). Here it boosts a traditional Italian pasta with clams in red sauce to another level.

# Spaghetti with Garlicky Clams in Red Sauce with Chili Crisp

SERVES 4 TO 6

12 ounces (340 g) spaghetti

3 cloves garlic, thinly sliced

3 tablespoons extra-virgin olive oil

2 heaping tablespoons (42 g) chili crisp, or more to taste

1 teaspoon dried oregano

½ cup (120 ml) dry white vermouth

1 cup (240 ml) passata

3 pounds (1.4 kg) littleneck or cherrystone clams (see Note, page 119)

Chopped fresh flat-leaf parsley, for garnish

In a large pot of boiling salted water, cook the pasta until al dente, 10 to 11 minutes. Reserve 1 cup (240 ml) of the pasta water before draining.

Meanwhile, in a large deep skillet or flameproof casserole, cook the garlic in the oil over medium heat until it just begins to color, 2 to 3 minutes. Stir in the chili crisp and oregano. Pour in the vermouth and boil for about 1 minute to reduce by one-third.

Add the passata and return to a boil. Add the clams, cover, and cook over high heat, stirring once, until the clams open, 3 to 5 minutes. Transfer the clams and their sauce to a large serving bowl. Add the drained pasta and toss to mix, adding as much of the reserved pasta water as needed to coat nicely. Garnish with chopped parsley.

**While sweet, succulent clams** lend their briny flavor to a wide range of preparations, the most common pairing is with red sauce, heavy on tomatoes, or a white sauce, with white wine laced with butter and garlic. Here we have clams with a twist of new taste. Susan douses the clams with a more complex flavor. Haul home some fresh clams and whip up the toasted garlic, almond, and basil pesto in little more than 5 minutes. And this pesto, spiked with lemon juice and a splash of balsamic vinegar, holds its bright flavor for several days.

# Linguine with Clams in Toasted Almond and Roasted Red Pepper Pesto

SERVES 4 TO 6

In a large pot of boiling salted water, cook the pasta until just al dente, 8 to 10 minutes. Reserve about ½ cup (120 ml) of the pasta water before draining.

Meanwhile, in a large deep skillet or flameproof casserole, heat the olive oil. Add the wine, 2 tablespoons of the parsley, and the hot pepper. When the wine reaches a full boil, add the clams, cover, and steam over high heat until they just open, 3 to 4 minutes. With a strainer or large slotted spoon, transfer the clams to a large serving bowl; cover with foil to keep warm. If any clams have not opened, give them another minute or two. Discard any that still don't open.

Stir the pesto into the liquid left in the pan. Add the cooked pasta and toss to coat. Simmer for 1 to 2 minutes, adding the reserved pasta water if needed. The dish should be a little saucy.

Pour the pasta and sauce over the clams, add the cheese, if using, and toss to mix. Garnish with the remaining tablespoon of parsley.

12 ounces (340 g) linguine

2 tablespoons extra-virgin olive oil

⅓ cup (80 ml) dry white wine

3 tablespoons coarsely chopped fresh flat-leaf parsley

¼ teaspoon crushed hot red pepper

3 pounds (1.4 kg) littleneck or cherrystone clams (see Note, page 119)

1 recipe Toasted Almond and Roasted Red Pepper Pesto (page 202)

⅓ cup (35 g) coarsely grated Asiago cheese (optional)

For many living in coastal areas, crab used to be taken for granted. A mound of claws piled on newspaper, beach roasts, fat crab cakes spiked with hot sauce, she-crab soup—abundance made us profligate. Now, with shortages, it has become a specialty item and quite expensive. Still, crab is worth the search, and there are reputable online sources. A little crab can make a big impact in pasta. The light sweetness, bite of arugula, and the brilliance of lemon in this recipe balance each other well.

# Capellini with Crab, Lemon, and Arugula

SERVES 4

12 ounces (340 g) capellini

5 tablespoons (70 g) unsalted butter

2 shallots, minced

1 pound (455 g) lump crab meat (see Note)

¼ cup (60 ml) dry white wine

½ cup (120 ml) fresh lemon juice

Grated zest of 1 lemon

¼ teaspoon crushed hot red pepper

Coarse salt and freshly ground black pepper

3 ounces (85 g) prewashed baby arugula (about 3 cups)

Grated Parmigiano Reggiano

In a large pot of boiling salted water, cook the pasta until al dente, about 5 minutes. Reserve ½ cup (120 ml) of the pasta water before draining.

Meanwhile, in a large skillet, melt the butter over medium heat. Add the shallots and cook for only a minute. Stir in the crab and toss to coat with butter. Add the white wine and bring to a boil. Reduce the heat to medium-low and stir in the lemon juice and zest. Season with the hot pepper, salt, and black pepper.

Add the drained pasta and arugula to the crab along with the reserved pasta water. Toss to mix. Pass the Parmigiano separately.

———

NOTE: Live crab or just-cooked crab claws are best, but they take time. Fresh lump crab is highly seasonal. When it's not available, opt for packaged lump crab in the refrigerator section at the seafood counter. Check the source and the harvest date—the fresher the better.

Many people who are otherwise picky about seafood sometimes love fried fish, which is why this recipe goes the extra mile. Nuggets of meaty halibut are coated with herbed panko and shallow-fried before being paired with the Mediterranean flavors of tomato, fennel, saffron, and anise in the form of Sambuca, the liqueur flavored with the essential oils of star anise. If you can find multicolored radiatori, the vegetable colors enhance the presentation even more, though the taste is the same.

# Radiatori with Fried Halibut, Fennel, Sambuca, and Saffron

SERVES 4

In a large pot of boiling salted water, cook the radiatori until al dente, 10 to 11 minutes. Reserve ½ cup (120 ml) of the pasta water before draining.

Meanwhile, in a large skillet, heat 3 tablespoons of the olive oil. Add the onion and fennel, toss with ½ teaspoon of the salt, cover, and cook over medium-high heat, stirring once or twice, until softened, about 3 minutes. Uncover, raise the heat to high, and sauté, stirring often, until the vegetables are soft and partially golden, about 3 minutes longer. Add the chopped tomatoes, reduce the heat to medium, and simmer for 2 to 3 minutes. Stir in the reserved pasta water, the Sambuca, and saffron.

While the sauce is cooking, fry the fish: On a plate, toss the panko with the thyme, marjoram, black pepper, cayenne, and the remaining ½ teaspoon salt. Dredge the fish cubes in the seasoned breadcrumbs to coat. In a medium cast-iron or heavy nonstick skillet, heat the remaining 3 tablespoons oil. Add the coated fish cubes and fry over medium-high heat, turning occasionally, until nicely browned, 3 to 4 minutes. If there are any crumbs left on the plate, throw them into the skillet.

To serve, in a large bowl, toss the pasta with the fennel sauce. Scatter the halibut and any crumbs in the pan over the top. Garnish generously with chopped parsley.

8 ounces (225 g) radiatori

6 tablespoons (90 ml) extra-virgin olive oil

1½ cups (170 g) thinly sliced onion

1½ cups (170 g) thinly sliced fresh fennel

1 teaspoon coarse salt

1½ cups (270 g) canned chopped tomatoes

1 tablespoon Sambuca or anisette

Pinch of saffron threads

⅓ cup (35 g) panko

½ teaspoon dried thyme

½ teaspoon dried marjoram

⅛ teaspoon freshly ground black pepper

Dash of cayenne pepper

8 ounces (225 g) skinless halibut, cut into ½-inch (1 cm) cubes

Chopped fresh flat-leaf parsley

This is a special occasion pasta, with a gorgeous presentation. Many markets sell both previously frozen and fresh lobster tails. Of course, fresh will impart more flavor, but both work quite well when doused in butter and flamed in cognac, as in this recipe. Take note of temperature; overcooked lobster has the texture of a rubber band. In general, Italians don't take to using cheese with seafood but will sometimes sprinkle some on lobster and crab pastas. Line up all the ingredients first; this needs to move quickly.

# Linguine with Lemony Lobster, Tomatoes, and Asparagus

SERVES 4

12 ounces (340 g) linguine

2 tablespoons extra-virgin olive oil

4 uncooked lobster tails (4 to 6 ounces each/115 to 170 g), split lengthwise in half, intestinal veins removed

1 bunch asparagus (about 1 pound/455 g), tough ends removed, stalks cut into 2-inch (5 cm) pieces

6 tablespoons (80 g) unsalted butter

Coarse salt and freshly ground black pepper

⅓ cup (80 ml) Cognac

¼ cup (60 ml) dry white wine or dry vermouth

12 to 14 cherry tomatoes, halved

⅓ cup (80 ml) heavy cream

2 tablespoons minced preserved lemon, or juice and grated zest of 1 lemon

2 tablespoons finely chopped fresh chives

¼ cup (25 g) grated Parmigiano Reggiano (optional)

In a large pot of boiling salted water, cook the pasta until al dente, 10 to 11 minutes; drain.

Meanwhile, in a large skillet, warm the olive oil over medium-high heat. Add the lobster tails, cut sides down, and sauté, turning once, until the shells turn bright red and the meat firms up just enough to remove from the shells, about 3 minutes. Transfer the lobster to a cutting board and let cool.

Steam the asparagus until crisp-tender and still bright green, about 3 minutes. Transfer to a bowl and toss with 2 tablespoons of the butter. Season lightly with salt and pepper and set aside.

As soon as the lobster is cool enough to handle, remove the meat from the shells and roughly chop into bite-size pieces or leave some tails whole, if preferred, as shown in the photo opposite. Reserve the shells for decorating the serving bowl, if you like.

Now the lobster is ready for its showtime. In a large skillet, melt the remaining 4 tablespoons (55 g) butter over medium heat. Add the lobster and stir to coat with the butter. Pour in the Cognac and carefully ignite it. When the flames subside, add the wine and boil for 30 to 60 seconds.

Add the tomatoes, cover the pan, and simmer over medium heat to heat through, about 2 minutes. Stir in the cream, lemon, and 1 tablespoon of the chives. Heat through. Taste to see if additional salt is needed.

Add the cooked pasta and asparagus to the lobster sauce. Gently toss to mix. Serve in a large bowl decorated with the shells, if you like. Sprinkle the Parmigiano on top, if using. Garnish with the remaining chives.

If you enjoy *moules frites*, chances are you'll adore Susan's mussels with pasta. Saffron was introduced to Italy by Spain in the thirteenth century. Growing the special crocus with saffron stigmas has a long heritage in Tuscany, and around Cortona there's been a revival of the tradition. Here, the mussels and saffron are paired with pasta to create a sumptuous black and yellow dish. Because mussel juices are quite salty, no extra salt is added. As with all shellfish, avoid overcooking to maintain tenderness. Another pasta suggestion: spaghetti alla chitarra.

# Spaghetti with Mussels in Saffron Cream

SERVES 4 TO 6

In a large pot of boiling salted water, cook the pasta until al dente, 9 to 10 minutes.

Meanwhile, in a large deep skillet, heat the olive oil. Add the shallot and cook over medium-high heat until softened, about 2 minutes. Pour in the vermouth; it will boil almost instantly. Add the mussels, cover, and cook, stirring once, until they just open, 3 to 5 minutes. Use a skimmer to remove the mussels to a bowl; discard any that do not open. If there is any grit at the bottom of the pan, strain the liquid into another skillet.

Add the cream, 2 tablespoons of the parsley, the saffron, and Sambuca, if using, to the liquid in the skillet. Bring to a boil. Using tongs, transfer the pasta to the cream sauce; toss to mix well.

Return the mussels to the pan and toss to mix with the pasta. Cover and cook over medium heat for about 1 minute to heat through. Serve directly from the skillet or transfer to a large serving bowl. Garnish with the remaining tablespoon chopped parsley.

12 ounces (340 g) spaghetti

2 tablespoons extra-virgin olive oil

1 large shallot, finely chopped

⅓ cup (80 ml) dry vermouth

3 pounds (1.4 kg) mussels, rinsed and scrubbed

⅓ cup (80 ml) heavy cream

3 tablespoons chopped fresh flat-leaf parsley

½ teaspoon saffron threads

1 tablespoon Sambuca or anisette (optional)

Here is a lovely way to serve salmon, with the pastel coral pink of the fish and green of the asparagus punctuated with bright red tomatoes and slivers of shiitakes. In Italy, cheese is not usually served with fish, but here it adds extra umami flavor to the delicate dish.

# Farfalle with Salmon, Asparagus, and Shiitake Mushrooms

SERVES 4 TO 6

12 ounces (340 g) farfalle

1 bunch asparagus (about 1 pound/500 g), tough ends removed, stalks cut into 1-inch (2.5 cm) pieces

1 pound (500 g) center-cut salmon fillet, skinned

½ teaspoon ground coriander

Coarse salt and freshly ground black pepper

2 tablespoons extra-virgin olive oil

2 tablespoons unsalted butter

1 large shallot, finely chopped

8 ounces (250 g) shiitake mushrooms, stemmed, caps thinly sliced

⅓ cup (80 ml) heavy cream

2 tablespoons fresh lemon juice, plus 2 teaspoons grated zest

8 to 10 cherry or grape tomatoes, halved

⅓ cup (35 g) grated Parmigiano Reggiano

In a large pot of boiling salted water, cook the pasta until it is al dente, about 10 minutes. Use a skimmer to scoop the pasta into a colander. Add the asparagus to the boiling water and cook until just tender but still bright green, 2 to 3 minutes. Reserve 1 cup (240 ml) of the pasta water, then drain.

Meanwhile, season the salmon on both sides with the coriander and a generous sprinkling of salt and pepper. In a large nonstick or cast-iron skillet, heat 1 tablespoon of the olive oil. Sear the salmon over high heat for 1 to 2 minutes on each side, until lightly browned but rare in the center. It will finish cooking when combined with the pasta. Remove to a cutting board and cut into ½- to ¾-inch (1 to 2 cm) chunks.

In the same skillet, melt the butter in the remaining 1 tablespoon olive oil. Add the shallot and shiitake mushrooms and cook over medium heat, stirring occasionally, until they are tender, 2 to 3 minutes. Pour in the cream and lemon juice and bring to a boil, scraping up any browned bits from the bottom of the pan. Pour in ⅔ cup (160 ml) of the reserved pasta water.

Add the pasta, asparagus, salmon chunks, and cherry tomatoes to the pan; toss gently to mix. Cover and simmer, tossing once, until the salmon is cooked through to your liking, and the pasta is heated through, about 2 minutes. Stir in the grated cheese and sprinkle the lemon zest on top.

Scallops and corn—both sweet—are a natural combo. Zesty lime brings out the best of the pairing. Scallops come in all sizes, which does not affect their taste, but because they should be distributed throughout the dish, quarter or halve them if they are large, so they are roughly 1 inch (2.5 cm) in diameter. One of the shell-shaped pastas, *chiocciole*, like *lumache*, is another word for snails.

# Chiocciole with Scallops, Corn, and Lime

SERVES 4

8 ounces (225 g) chiocciole

2 tablespoons unsalted butter

2 tablespoons extra-virgin olive oil

12 ounces (140 g) small scallops, patted dry

1 medium shallot, finely chopped

½ red bell pepper, diced

½ cup (120 ml) dry white wine or dry vermouth

⅓ cup (80 ml) heavy cream

1 (11-ounce/310 g) can extra-sweet corn niblets, undrained

Juice of 1 lime (about 2 tablespoons)

Coarse salt and freshly ground black pepper

In a large pot of boiling salted water, cook the chiocciole until al dente, 9 to 10 minutes.

Meanwhile, in a large nonstick skillet, melt the butter in the olive oil over medium-high heat. Add the scallops and sauté, tossing, until lightly browned and done to your liking, about 4 minutes. With a slotted spoon, remove the scallops to a plate.

Add the shallot and bell pepper to the oil in the pan. Cook over medium heat, stirring often, until they are softened, about 2 minutes. Pour in the wine. As soon as it bubbles, reduce the heat to medium. Add the cream and cook, stirring to release all the browned bits around the pan.

Add the corn and any liquid from the can and the lime juice. Season with salt and pepper to taste. Return the scallops to the skillet and simmer for 1 to 2 minutes. Add the pasta, toss, and serve.

Like shrimp, these little scallops cook quickly, which makes them perfect for a *pasta veloce*. Plum tomatoes, punched up with a dab of tomato paste to enhance their flavor, create a light sauce that doesn't overwhelm the seafood. Crisp toasted breadcrumbs, sprinkled on top of the finished dish and tossed just before serving, provide a textural counterpoint to tender scallops and pasta.

# Linguine with Bay Scallops in Fresh Tomato Sauce

SERVES 4 TO 6

In a large saucepan of boiling salted water, cook the linguine until just barely al dente, 8 to 9 minutes. Reserve ½ cup (120 ml) of the pasta water before draining.

Meanwhile, in a large nonstick skillet, heat 2 tablespoons of the olive oil over medium heat. Add the breadcrumbs and cook, tossing, until lightly browned and toasted, about 3 minutes. Scrape into a bowl and season with ¼ teaspoon of the salt, ⅛ teaspoon pepper, and 1 tablespoon each of the basil and parsley. Wipe out the pan.

In the same skillet, melt the butter in the remaining 2 tablespoons olive oil over medium heat. Add the shallot, garlic, marjoram, and hot pepper. Cook, stirring, until the shallot and garlic are softened but not browned, 2 to 3 minutes. Add the tomatoes and remaining ¼ teaspoon salt and ⅛ teaspoon pepper, raise the heat to high, and sauté, stirring often, until the tomatoes soften, about 3 minutes. Pour in the vermouth and cook for 1 minute longer.

Add the scallops to the tomato sauce, reduce the heat to medium, and simmer for 1 minute. Add the pasta, reserved pasta water, and remaining 2 tablespoons each basil and parsley. Simmer, tossing once or twice, until the pasta has absorbed most of the liquid and the scallops are cooked through, about 2 minutes. Transfer to a large serving bowl and sprinkle the toasted breadcrumbs on top.

------

NOTE: Bay scallops are small, roughly ½ inch (12 mm) in diameter. If they are not available, you can use larger scallops halved or quartered, depending on size.

8 ounces (225 g) linguine

¼ cup (60 ml) extra-virgin olive oil

½ cup (50 g) fresh breadcrumbs or panko

½ teaspoon coarse salt

¼ teaspoon freshly ground black pepper

3 tablespoons slivered fresh basil

3 tablespoons chopped fresh flat-leaf parsley

2 tablespoons unsalted butter

1 medium shallot, thinly sliced

2 cloves garlic, thinly sliced

½ teaspoon dried marjoram

¼ teaspoon crushed hot red pepper

4 large plum tomatoes, diced

⅓ cup (80 ml) dry vermouth or dry white wine

12 ounces (340 g) bay scallops (see Note)

For Michelin-starred chef Silvia Baracchi in Cortona, whose red wine pasta is included on page 177, every recipe should surprise your taste buds as well as delight the eye. In this one, green olives provide a piquant bed for twirled spaghetti, bathed in sweet red vermouth. Her plates often pop with the added color of edible flowers—tiny pansies, borage, chamomile. At her sybaritic greenhouse restaurant, Silvia tops the pasta with a special catch of raw shrimp. In our version, we poach them briefly, then coat lightly with olive oil. To present the spaghetti as shown in the photo, use a large ladle and long fork or narrow tongs to scoop up and twirl a portion of the pasta, as if you were making a nest. As you lower the spaghetti onto the plate, pull gently to form an elongated shape.

# Spaghetti in Red Vermouth with Shrimp and Green Olive Sauce

**SERVES 4 AS A FIRST COURSE**

9 ounces (255 g) spaghetti

8 ounces (225 g) shelled and deveined shrimp (see Note)

5 tablespoons (75 ml) extra-virgin olive oil

Coarse salt and freshly ground black pepper

2 cloves garlic, crushed through a press

1 teaspoon minced fresh red chile pepper, or ¼ teaspoon crushed dried hot pepper

½ teaspoon fresh thyme leaves, plus several sprigs for garnish

½ cup (120 ml) sweet vermouth

Green Olive Sauce (page 136)

In a large pot of boiling salted water, cook the pasta until al dente, about 10 minutes. At the same time, bring a medium saucepan of water to a boil.

Add the shrimp to the smaller pot of boiling water and cook for 1 to 2 minutes, just until pink and loosely curled. Drain immediately. Finely dice the shrimp, toss with 1 tablespoon of the olive oil, and season lightly with salt and black pepper.

When the pasta is almost done, in a large skillet, heat the remaining ¼ cup (60 ml) olive oil with the garlic, chile pepper, and thyme leaves. Sauté over medium-high heat for 30 to 60 seconds, until the garlic is softened and fragrant, then pour in the vermouth and add ¼ teaspoon salt. Boil for 1 minute to reduce slightly.

As soon as the pasta is al dente, drain and add to the skillet; toss to coat. Simmer for a minute or two, tossing occasionally to allow the pasta to absorb the vermouth.

To serve, spread 2 tablespoons of the olive sauce on 4 individual plates. Top with a swirl of pasta and spoon the shrimp on top (see Note). Garnish with sprigs of thyme.

———

**NOTE:** Since they are being diced, the size of the shrimp doesn't matter here, but quality does. Buy the freshest, sweetest shrimp, preferably wild caught.

Buttery, pungent Castelvetrano olives from Sicily are available in many markets and online. If they're not pitted, it's quick work to lay the olives down on a cutting board and smash them with the flat side of a chef's knife. The pit will pop right out. For the recipe on page 134, you can make the olive sauce a day ahead and let it return to room temperature before using, or prepare it while the pasta cooks. The olive sauce recipe can be doubled or tripled if you want to have this on hand to spread on crackers or crostini.

# GREEN OLIVE SAUCE

MAKES ½ CUP (120 ML)

3½ ounces (100 g) green Castelvetrano olives, pitted

2 tablespoons olive brine

1 tablespoon extra-virgin olive oil

Freshly ground black pepper

In a mini processor or blender, puree half the olives with the brine and the olive oil. If using olives without brine, add a little water and a pinch of salt. Finely chop the rest of the olives and stir them all together in a small bowl. Season with a generous grind of pepper. Store in a covered jar in the refrigerator for up to 5 days.

On a warm day, this cooling salad stars at a summer lunch party. Serve on a bed of butter lettuce or arugula. A 6- to 8-ounce (170 to 225 g) slab of baked or poached salmon from the deli, or whipped up in 7 minutes in your toaster oven or air-fryer, would make a pretty accompaniment to the shellfish. Serve with chilled rosé.

# Penne Seafood Salad

SERVES 4 TO 6

In a large pot of boiling salted water, cook the penne until al dente, 10 to 11 minutes. Drain and rinse under cold running water to cool; drain well.

As soon as you put on the pasta water, in a heavy medium saucepan, combine the white wine with the bay leaf, lemon slice, garlic, and ⅔ cup (160 ml) water over medium-high heat. Bring to a simmer, cover, reduce the heat to medium-low, and steep for 3 minutes. Add the shrimp and scallops to the liquid, cover, and simmer, stirring once or twice, until the seafood is cooked through and white in the center, about 4 minutes. Remove the shrimp and scallops with a slotted spoon and reserve the broth. Discard the bay leaf, lemon, and garlic.

In a small bowl, whisk together the mayonnaise and sour cream until blended. Mix in ⅓ cup (80 ml) of the reserved seafood broth and the lemon juice. Season the dressing with salt and pepper.

Put the shrimp and scallops in a large bowl, tearing the shrimp into bite-size pieces, if you like. Add the celery, cherry tomatoes, and the pasta. Pour the dressing over everything, and toss to coat evenly. Serve at once or lightly chilled.

---

NOTE: If all you have are frozen shrimp and scallops, throw them right into the wine broth and cook for 3 to 5 minutes longer, until they are done.

8 ounces (225 g) penne

⅔ cup (160 ml) dry white wine

1 bay leaf

1 thick slice lemon, plus 2 tablespoons fresh lemon juice

1 clove garlic, smashed

1 pound (450 g) shelled and deveined shrimp (see Note)

8 ounces (225 g) scallops, halved if large (see Note)

½ cup (120 g) mayonnaise

⅓ cup (80 ml) sour cream

Coarse salt and freshly ground black pepper

2 large stalks celery, diced

½ pint box (.5 liter) cherry tomatoes, halved

In Italy, with its 4,700 miles (7,600 km) of coastline, naturally seafood reigns. So many tasty spiny lobsters, varieties of shrimp, langoustines, on and on, are served forth with gusto at places such as La Pineta, smack on the sea in Marina di Bibbona, Tuscany. Picture a beach shack with crystal glasses and over-the-top service. Everyone raves about this recipe, which is perfect for dining seaside or a dinner party at home. The photo shows dramatic giant-size shells, but any size shell will do. Same with the shrimp size—whatever type, bathing them in buttery garlic sauce signals irresistible eating. Accompany with great bread to sop up all the juices.

# Conchiglie with Garlicky Shrimp

SERVES 4

In a large pot of boiling salted water, cook the pasta until it is al dente, 10 to 11 minutes, or a bit longer if you have the very large shells. Drain into a colander.

Meanwhile, heat a large deep skillet, preferably cast-iron, over high heat until smoking hot. Add the olive oil and let heat through. Add the shrimp and sear until pink, curled, and lightly browned around the edges, 1 to 1½ minutes per side. Remove to a plate with a slotted spoon or skimmer. Reduce the heat to low.

Add the chopped garlic, oregano, and hot pepper to the oil in the skillet and cook, stirring, until the garlic is softened and fragrant, 1 to 2 minutes. Pour in the vermouth, raise the heat to medium, and boil until reduced to ½ cup, 1 to 2 minutes. Stir in the lemon juice.

Mash the crushed raw garlic with the butter; it needn't be smooth. Return the shrimp to the skillet and add the cooked pasta and garlic butter. Toss until the butter is melted and the shrimp and sauce are mixed with the pasta. Season with salt and black pepper.

10 ounces (280 g) conchiglie

⅓ cup (80 ml) extra-virgin olive oil

1¼ pounds (565 g) shelled and deveined shrimp, patted dry

7 cloves garlic (6 chopped, 1 crushed through a press)

1 teaspoon dried oregano

1 teaspoon crushed hot red pepper

⅔ cup (120 ml) dry vermouth or dry white wine

2 tablespoons fresh lemon juice

4 tablespoons (55 g/ ¼ stick) unsalted butter, cut into pieces

Coarse salt and freshly ground black pepper

*Sausage gives this pasta* a big plus in texture and piquancy. Even with a spicy Italian sausage, the heat level can vary wildly from brand to brand. That's why we suggest seasoning the dish to your taste at the end. Or simply use sweet Italian sausage and black pepper only.

# Cavatappi with Shrimp, Spicy Sausage, and White Beans

SERVES 6

12 ounces (340 g) cavatappi

¼ cup (60 ml) extra-virgin olive oil

1 pound (450 g) shelled and deveined shrimp, patted dry

1 onion, thinly sliced

½ teaspoon coarse salt

3 or 4 cloves garlic, thinly sliced

10 to 12 ounces (275 to 340 g) hot Italian sausage, casing removed

1 teaspoon dried oregano

1 pound (500 g) fresh plum tomatoes, diced, or 2 cups (250 g) chopped canned tomatoes

1 (15½-ounce/440 g) can cannellini or Great Northern white beans, rinsed and drained

3 tablespoons coarsely chopped fresh flat-leaf parsley

Freshly ground black pepper and crushed hot red pepper

In a large pot of boiling salted water, cook the pasta until it is just barely al dente, 10 to 12 minutes. Do not drain.

Meanwhile, in a large deep skillet or flameproof casserole, heat 2 tablespoons of the olive oil. When it is very hot, add the shrimp and sauté them over high heat for 1 minute on each side to brown lightly; they'll finish cooking in the sauce. Remove to a plate.

Add the remaining 2 tablespoons olive oil to the pan along with the sliced onion. Season with the salt. Sauté over high heat, stirring, for 2 to 3 minutes to soften. Add the garlic and sauté for another minute. Reduce the heat to medium-high.

Add the sausage and use a large spoon to break up the meat into small chunks. Season with the oregano and cook, stirring, until the sausage is no longer pink, about 3 minutes. Add the tomatoes and cook for about 2 minutes, until they just soften.

As soon as the pasta is al dente, scoop it into the sauce in the pan along with 1 cup (240 ml) of the pasta water. Simmer for 2 minutes. Stir in the beans and parsley. Season with additional salt if needed and with both freshly ground black and hot pepper to taste.

**Squid ink pasta is** startlingly black. A staple in the Veneto area, it's often served with shrimp, cuttlefish, and, what else, squid, aka calamari. While the ink doesn't change the flavor of the pasta significantly, it does lend a mild briny overtone and results in a chewy texture. Most of all, it looks dramatic with the pale shellfish, colorful tomatoes, and green herbs.

# Squid Ink Spaghetti with a Trio of Seafood

SERVES 4

In a large pot of boiling salted water, cook the pasta until al dente, about 10 minutes.

Meanwhile, in a large flameproof casserole, heat ¼ cup (60 ml) of the olive oil over medium-high heat. Add the shrimp and sear for about 1 minute on each side, just to add some color. They will finish cooking later. Remove to a plate.

Add the scallops to the pan and brown lightly, 1½ to 2 minutes on each side. Remove to the plate. Reduce the heat to medium-low.

Add the garlic, anchovy paste, and hot pepper to the oil in the pan. Cook, stirring occasionally, until the garlic just starts to color, about 2 minutes. Immediately pour in the wine and add the salt. Bring to a boil, reduce the heat, and simmer for 1 to 2 minutes. Return the shrimp and scallops to the pan along with any juices that have accumulated on the plate. Simmer for 2 minutes to finish cooking the seafood.

Add the calamari, cook for only 30 seconds, drizzle on the remaining olive oil, then add the pasta, tomatoes, and basil. Toss over the heat for 1 minute to mix, then serve at once.

———

**NOTE:** Squid ink pasta is a little hard to find in markets. If you order online, either spaghetti or linguine is fine.

12 ounces (340 g) squid ink spaghetti (see Note)

⅓ cup (80 ml) extra-virgin olive oil

1 pound (450 g) shelled and deveined shrimp, patted dry

½ pound (225 g) medium-size scallops, patted dry

6 cloves garlic, thinly sliced

1½ teaspoons anchovy paste

¾ teaspoon crushed hot red pepper, or more to taste

1 cup (240 ml) dry white wine

½ teaspoon coarse salt

¼ pound (110 g) calamari tubes, cut into rings

2 cups (225 g) tiny tomatoes, preferably a mix of red and yellow

2 tablespoons slivered fresh basil or coarsely chopped flat-leaf parsley

It's always fun to see a huge swordfish, with its menacing appendage, propped up on ice at the Venice fish market. Swordfish steaks are often grilled, but in this recipe, bite-size pieces are quickly seared, locking in the tender, mild sweetness. Bright orange zest and a splash of wine heighten the delicate flavor, while small capers add their sharper punch.

# Tagliatelle with Swordfish, Chickpeas, Spinach, and Orange Zest

SERVES 4

12 ounces (340 g) tagliatelle

5 ounces (140 g) frozen chopped spinach

Coarse salt and freshly ground black pepper

¼ cup (60 ml) extra-virgin olive oil

2 bay leaves

2 small swordfish steaks about 1 inch (2.5 cm) thick (7 ounces/200 g each), cut into bite-size cubes

¼ cup (60 ml) dry white wine

Grated zest of 1 orange, plus a few long strips

¼ cup (60 ml) fresh orange juice

1 (15½-ounce/440 g) can chickpeas, rinsed and drained

1 tablespoon tiny nonpareil brined capers

In a large pot of salted water, cook the pasta until al dente, 4 to 5 minutes. Reserve 1 cup (240 ml) of the pasta water.

Meanwhile, drop the frozen spinach into a medium saucepan of boiling water. Throw in a little salt and pepper. Reduce the heat to a simmer, cover, and cook for 3 minutes. Drain into a fine sieve and run under cold water to cool. Squeeze out the excess water. (Cook the spinach in a microwave according to directions if you prefer.)

In a large skillet, heat the olive oil with the bay leaves over high heat. When very hot, add the swordfish pieces and toss to quickly sear all over, about 2 minutes. Add the wine and let it come to a quick boil. Immediately reduce the heat to medium and cook the swordfish until it is firm and white throughout, about 2 minutes. Add the orange zest and juice. Discard the bay leaves. Stir in the chickpeas, capers, and spinach. Season with salt and pepper to taste.

When the pasta is al dente, transfer it with tongs directly to the skillet. Add the reserved pasta water and simmer for 2 to 3 more minutes to blend the flavors. Serve in shallow bowls, garnished with strips of orange zest.

**Easy to double, this** travels well. Pack it into your basket for a tailgate, potluck, or beach picnic. Take along a good loaf and a chilled rosé.

# Mediterranean Elbow Macaroni Salad with Tuna, Fennel, Bell Pepper, and Red Onion

**SERVES 3 OR 4**

¾ cup (75 g) finely diced red onion

½ teaspoon coarse salt

2 tablespoons fresh lemon juice

6 ounces (170 g) elbow macaroni

12 large pitted Kalamata or Gaeta olives

1 tablespoon tiny nonpareil brined capers

⅓ cup (80 ml) extra-virgin olive oil

¼ cup (5 g) lightly packed fresh basil or flat-leaf parsley

Freshly ground black pepper

1 cup (100 g) diced fresh fennel

1 cup (100 g) diced red bell pepper

1 (5-ounce/141 g) can solid light tuna packed in oil, drained

In a small sieve, rinse the onion briefly under cold running water; drain well (see Note). Put the onion in a bowl and toss with the salt and 1 tablespoon of the lemon juice. Set aside.

In a large pot of boiling salted water, cook the macaroni until al dente, about 7 minutes; drain.

In a food processor, combine the olives, capers, olive oil, basil, remaining 1 tablespoon lemon juice, and a generous grind of black pepper. Pulse until the olives are chopped and the dressing is emulsified, about 12 times.

In a large bowl, combine the fennel, red bell pepper, and cooked macaroni. Add the red onions with any liquid that remains in the bowl and flake the tuna in large chunks on top. Toss briefly to mix. Pour on the olive dressing and toss to coat. Serve at room temperature or lightly chilled.

———

**NOTE:** Rinsing onion under water removes much of the raw bite, especially when it is then tossed with salt and lemon juice.

Fresh tuna is delicate but meaty. Here, it attains culinary-star status with sun-dried tomatoes and olives—colorful and tantalizing. Just two servings of fatty fish a week is more beneficial in boosting omega-3s than even the best fish oil.

# Torchietti with Fresh Tuna, Olives, and Sun-Dried Tomatoes

SERVES 4

In a large pot of boiling salted water, cook the pasta until just al dente, about 10 minutes. Reserve 1 cup (240 ml) of the pasta water before draining.

Meanwhile, season the tuna on both sides with salt and pepper. In a large nonstick skillet, heat 1 tablespoon of the olive oil and sear the fish over high heat for 1½ to 2 minutes on each side to brown lightly, leaving the inside very rare; it will finish cooking later. Remove to a cutting board and carve into large chunks.

In the same skillet, heat the remaining 3 tablespoons oil. Add the shallot and garlic and cook over medium heat until soft, about 2 minutes. Stir in the anchovy paste, hot pepper, and thyme. Pour in the wine and bring to a boil over medium-high heat. Add the lemon juice, olives, sun-dried tomatoes, and ½ cup (120 ml) of the reserved pasta water.

Add the pasta to the sauce and simmer for 1 to 2 minutes, stirring and adding more pasta water if needed to moisten. Add the tuna chunks and simmer, tossing gently, until the fish is cooked to your taste, 1 to 2 minutes. Serve with an extra drizzle of olive oil. Garnish with thyme and citrus.

8 ounces (225 g) torchietti

12 ounces (340 g) fresh tuna, preferably sushi-grade yellowtail, cut about ¾ inch (2 cm) thick

Coarse salt and freshly ground black pepper

¼ cup (60 ml) extra-virgin olive oil, plus a drizzle more

1 medium shallot, thinly sliced

2 cloves garlic, finely chopped

1 teaspoon anchovy paste

¼ teaspoon crushed hot red pepper

½ teaspoon dried thyme

½ cup (120 ml) dry white wine

1 tablespoon fresh lemon juice

½ cup (60 g) pitted Kalamata or Gaeta olives

½ cup (60 g) pitted Castelvetrano or other brined green olives

½ cup (28 g) oil-packed sun-dried tomato strips

Fresh thyme sprigs, lime and orange slices, for garnish

This recipe comes right out of the pantry. While the usual version contains only anchovies, Susan's addition of good canned tuna turns it into a rich and substantial main course. Canned tuna plays a huge role in the history of Italian fishing. It's fascinating to visit the many fishing villages, such as the charming Marzamemi in Sicily with its Arabic courtyards, and colorful Carloforte in Sardinia, where tuna was once the main livelihood. Remnants of the processing plants are falling to ruin, although a few are being restored. At Favignana in the Aegadian Islands, displays show where tuna was first boiled, dried, then canned. Deep in the history of these villages lies the memory of the annual *tonnara*, meaning "trap." Vast numbers of tuna were caught in elaborate nets, then rounded up between boats.

# Spaghettini alla Puttanesca

SERVES 4

12 ounces (340 g) spaghettini

3 cloves garlic, thinly sliced

¼ cup (60 ml) extra-virgin olive oil

3 tablespoons tiny nonpareil brined capers

6 anchovy fillets, coarsely chopped

¼ to ½ teaspoon crushed hot red pepper, to taste

1 (28-ounce/790 g) can chopped tomatoes

12 pitted Kalamata or Gaeta olives, quartered

Coarse salt and freshly ground black pepper

1 (5-ounce/141 g) can solid light tuna in oil, drained

3 tablespoons coarsely chopped fresh basil or flat-leaf parsley, plus more for garnish

In a large pot of boiling salted water, cook the spaghettini until just barely al dente, about 7 minutes.

Meanwhile, in a large deep skillet or flameproof casserole, cook the garlic in the olive oil over medium heat until softened and fragrant, about 2 minutes. Add the capers, anchovies, and hot pepper. Cook, stirring, until the anchovies dissolve, about 1 minute.

Add the tomatoes with their juices and the olives. Raise the heat to medium-high and bring to a boil. Cook, uncovered, for 5 minutes to reduce slightly. Season with salt and black pepper to taste.

As soon as the pasta is almost al dente, use tongs to add it to the sauce. Simmer until the pasta has absorbed a bit of the sauce and is al dente, about 2 minutes. Add the tuna and basil or parsley and toss to mix in and break up the tuna. Transfer to a large serving bowl and garnish with additional chopped basil or parsley.

Bottarga, the salted, pressed, and dried roe of red mullet or tuna, is very popular in Sicily. It is available in many markets and online. Before opening, it is shelf stable and does not require refrigeration. After opening, store in the fridge and it will last for several months. While most recipes call for simply grating it, keeping some in small bits delivers a bigger hit of briny flavor. Peel off the thin membrane that surrounds the roe. It's easiest to grate the bottarga on a Microplane.

# Spaghettini with Bottarga in Garlic Lemon Cream

**SERVES 4 AS A FIRST COURSE**

In a large pot of boiling salted water, cook the spaghettini until al dente, 6 to 7 minutes; drain.

Meanwhile, in a small heavy saucepan, combine the cream, garlic, and lemon zest. Bring to a boil, reduce the heat to low, and simmer for 8 to 10 minutes to thicken to a coating consistency. Stir in the lemon juice. Season lightly with salt and pepper.

Transfer pasta to a large serving bowl. Pour on the sauce, add the bottarga and 2 tablespoons of the parsley, and toss to mix well. Garnish with the remaining tablespoon of parsley.

8 ounces (225 g) spaghettini

1 cup (240 ml) heavy cream

2 cloves garlic, crushed through a press

1 teaspoon grated lemon zest

1 tablespoon fresh lemon juice

Coarse salt and freshly ground black pepper

2 ounces (55 g) bottarga, peeled (see headnote), half grated, half very finely diced

3 tablespoons chopped fresh flat-leaf parsley

# Meat and Poultry

Just like the eponymous sandwich that inspired Susan to make this pasta, the key to success is stellar ingredients: deeply flavored hickory-smoked bacon, the bite of arugula, and juicy tomatoes. Because the tomatoes are not really cooked, just warmed through, choose the best—ripe and bursting with flavor.

# BLT Spaghetti

SERVES 4 TO 6

12 ounces (340 g) spaghetti

10 ounces (280 g) bacon, cut crosswise into ½-inch (1 cm) strips

3 tablespoons extra-virgin olive oil

1 onion, thinly sliced

½ teaspoon coarse salt

¼ teaspoon sugar

Generous grind of black pepper

1 to 1¼ pounds (450 g to 570 g) tomatoes, cut into ¾- to 1-inch (2 to 2.5 cm) chunks

3 cups (about 2 ounces/ 55 g) lightly packed arugula

Finely shredded Asiago cheese

In a large pot of boiling salted water, cook the spaghetti until al dente, 9 to 10 minutes. Reserve 1 cup (240 ml) of the pasta water before draining.

Meanwhile, in a large deep skillet, cook the bacon in 1 tablespoon of the olive oil over medium heat, stirring to separate the pieces, until the fat renders and the bacon is lightly browned, about 3 minutes. Transfer the bacon to a paper towel.

Drain off all but about 1 tablespoon fat from the pan. Add the remaining 2 tablespoons olive oil and the onion. Season with the salt, sugar, and pepper. Cook over medium-high heat, stirring often, until the onion is golden brown, 4 to 5 minutes. Stir in ½ cup (120 ml) of the reserved pasta water.

Toss the cooked spaghetti with the liquid and onion in the pan to coat. Add the tomatoes, arugula, and bacon, and toss to mix evenly, including the remaining pasta water, if needed, to moisten. Serve with a sprinkling of Asiago cheese.

Unsmoked scarmorza cheese is a toasty white, while the smoked is the color of a russet pear, which shape it also resembles. Tied off at the top so it can hang to age, the double-ball scarmoza also looks like a roly-poly little priest's cassock and melts easily. On winter nights, Ed often melts the smoked variety in a skillet over coals in the fireplace, then grills some bread to dip into the cheese. It's easy to order, but if necessary, substitute smoked mozzarella, quite similar in taste and method of preparation. Since the strength of truffle oil can vary, taste before adding the second spoonful. Alternative pastas: cavatappi or fusilli.

# Casarecce with Bacon, Savoy Cabbage, Smoked Scarmorza, and Truffle Oil

SERVES 4

In a large pot of boiling salted water, cook the pasta until al dente, 9 to 11 minutes. Reserve ½ cup (120 ml) of the pasta water before draining.

Meanwhile, steam the cabbage until it is tender but still maintains a little crunch, about 4 minutes. Set aside.

Shake the bacon cubes in a bag with the flour to coat lightly. In a large skillet, heat the olive oil. Add the bacon cubes and fry over medium-high heat, stirring often, until lightly browned and crisp on the outside, 3 to 4 minutes. With a slotted spoon, remove to a paper towel.

Ladle the reserved pasta water into the skillet. Add the scarmorza, reduce the heat to medium-low, and simmer, stirring, until the cheese melts, 3 to 4 minutes. Mix in the cabbage and bacon and season with salt and pepper. Add the pasta and drizzle on the truffle oil. Toss and serve.

12 ounces (340 g) casarecce

½ head Savoy cabbage (about 1½ pounds/680 g), shredded

8 ounces (225 g) lean slab bacon, cut into small cubes

2 tablespoons all-purpose flour

5 tablespoons (75 ml) extra-virgin olive oil

6 ounces (170 g) smoked scarmorza cheese, cut into small cubes

Coarse salt and freshly ground black pepper

2 teaspoons white truffle oil (see Note, page 91)

At La Gensola, a righteous trattoria in Rome, their Amatriciana pulls in the crowds. All over Rome, this recipe is beloved, and theirs is one of the best. *Guanciale* is cured pig cheek, the meat traditionally used in this recipe for its savory fat. The origin story recalls shepherds in the hills above the town of Amatrice in Lazio. Their staple was hunks of guanciale and some cheese. Perhaps apocryphal, the preference for hollow *bucatini*, meaning "little hole," comes from these shepherds wrapping pasta dough around wire. The town of Norcia in Umbria is famous for all kinds of traditional *salume*, including wild boar and guanciale. It's a favorite spring weekend destination for Italians, not only for a great lunch on the piazza but for the leisurely walks in stupendous fields of wildflowers. If you can't find guanciale, use pancetta, but don't tell anyone from Amatrice. Rigatoni or spaghetti will substitute.

# Bucatini all'Amatriciana

SERVES 4 TO 6

12 ounces (340 g) bucatini

2 tablespoons extra-virgin olive oil

4 ounces (115 g) guanciale, cut crosswise into ¼-inch (6 mm) thick strips

⅓ cup (80 ml) dry white wine

1 (14-ounce/400 g) can San Marzano tomatoes, drained (about 1½ cups)

½ teaspoon crushed hot red pepper

Pinch of sugar

Coarse salt

⅔ cup (60 g) shredded pecorino Romano

In a large pot of boiling salted water, cook the bucatini until just barely al dente, 9 to 11 minutes. Reserve 1 cup (240 ml) of the pasta water before draining.

Meanwhile, heat 1 tablespoon of the olive oil in a large deep skillet. Add the guanciale and cook over medium heat, stirring occasionally, until the guanciale renders some of its fat and turns light golden, 3 to 5 minutes. Pour in the wine, increase the heat, and boil until it is reduced to a syrup. With a slotted spoon, remove the guanciale to a plate. Pour the liquid in the pan into a small bowl.

Add the remaining 1 tablespoon olive oil to the pan set over medium-high heat. Add the tomatoes, squeezing them through your fingers to mash them. Add 3 tablespoons of the reserved fat and wine, the hot pepper, and sugar. Sauté until the tomatoes are reduced to a jammy consistency, about 3 minutes. Ladle about ⅔ cup (160 ml) of the pasta water into the tomatoes and adjust the salt.

When the bucatini is almost al dente, use tongs to transfer it into the sauce. Add half the guanciale and simmer the sauce, tossing, until the pasta is al dente, about 2 minutes. Mix in half the cheese and divide the pasta among shallow pasta bowls. Sprinkle the remaining cheese and the rest of the guanciale on top.

Mild and creamy, this pasta is comfort food. Semi-soft, young Fontina cheese melts beautifully to create the smooth sauce. The best Fontina comes from Val d'Aosta in the overwhelmingly beautiful northwest mountains, one of the best summer hiking and winter sports areas in Italy. In dreamy Cogne, cozy village restaurant Brasserie du Bon Bec serves melted Fontina with squares of polenta to dip. While Italian Fontina has a distinctive nutty taste, it is sometimes hard to come by. The internet to the rescue! Domestic Fontina, made with pasteurized milk, is pleasing, but quite mild. A bit of added Parmigiano punches up the flavor.

# Farfalle with Ham, Mushrooms, and Peas in Creamy Fontina Sauce

SERVES 4 TO 5

In a large pot of boiling salted water, cook the farfalle until al dente, 8 to 10 minutes. Place the frozen peas in a large colander; rinse briefly to break up any clumps.

Meanwhile, in a heavy medium saucepan, combine the milk, cream, nutmeg, and cayenne. Bring to a boil over medium heat, stirring and scraping the bottom often. As soon as bubbles appear around the edges, reduce the heat to medium-low. Gradually whisk in the dissolved potato starch and simmer, whisking, until thickened, 1 to 2 minutes. Remove from the heat and add the Fontina, stirring until it melts. Season with salt and black pepper. Set the cheese sauce aside, covered to keep warm.

In a large deep skillet, sauté the shallot and mushrooms in the olive oil over high heat, stirring and tossing often, until the mushrooms start to give up their liquid and are just beginning to color, about 3 minutes. Season with the lemon juice, salt, and a generous grind of black pepper. Add the ham, remove from the heat, and cover to keep warm.

When the farfalle is al dente, drain into the colander right over the peas. Add the pasta and peas and the cheese sauce to the skillet. Sprinkle on the Parmigiano and toss to mix everything together.

10 ounces (280 g) farfalle

1 cup (8 ounces/225 g) frozen baby peas

1 cup (240 ml) whole milk

½ cup (120 ml) heavy cream

¼ teaspoon freshly grated nutmeg

⅛ teaspoon cayenne pepper

1½ teaspoons potato starch, or cornstarch dissolved in 2 tablespoons water

3 ounces (85 g) Fontina cheese, shredded (about ¾ cup)

Coarse salt and freshly ground black pepper

1 shallot, chopped

8 ounces (225 g) white button or baby bella (cremini) mushrooms, thickly sliced

3 tablespoons extra-virgin olive oil

2 teaspoons fresh lemon juice

8 ounces (225 g) flavorful ham, cubed

3 tablespoons grated Parmigiano Reggiano

This pasta gets its smoky and aromatic flavor from the pancetta and the generous amount of fresh rosemary that suffuses the so-easy sauce. If *pancetta affumicata* is unavailable, use a hickory-smoked bacon. Penne is also a natural partner to this recipe.

# Bucatini al Fumo

SERVES 4 TO 6

12 ounces (340 g) bucatini

8 ounces (225 g) smoked pancetta, finely chopped

¼ cup (60 ml) extra-virgin olive oil

1 onion, chopped

2 cloves garlic, minced

1 teaspoon chopped fresh rosemary

⅓ cup (80 ml) dry white wine

¼ cup (60 ml) tomato paste

1 cup (250 g) diced canned tomatoes, preferably Roma

⅓ cup (80 ml) heavy cream

Coarse salt and freshly ground black pepper

Grated Parmigiano Reggiano

In a large pot of boiling salted water, cook the bucatini until al dente, 9 to 11 minutes; drain.

Meanwhile, in a large skillet, cook the pancetta in the olive oil over medium-high heat, stirring, until crisp, 3 to 4 minutes. Remove the pancetta with a slotted spoon and drain on paper towels. Remove all but 3 tablespoons fat from the pan.

Add the onion to the skillet and sauté, stirring, until softened and golden, about 3 minutes. Add the rosemary and wine, bring to a boil, then reduce the heat to medium. Stir in the tomato paste, tomatoes, and cream. Season with salt and pepper. Simmer for 3 to 4 minutes to blend the flavors.

Add the bucatini and pancetta to the sauce. Toss to mix well. Serve in bowls. Pass the Parmigiano on the side.

Corkscrew pasta sinks its curly ridges into this well-balanced pasta sauce. Pecorino, a sheep's milk cheese, is one of the greats of Italy. The cheese is sold in four stages, including *semi-stagionato*, aged three to five months, which is great for cooking as well as for the antipasto platter. Some cheesemongers carry this full-flavored pecorino, mostly from Tuscany and Sardinia. If you go to Tuscany, don't miss the Renaissance town of Pienza, with its many pecorino shops and farms. It is legal to bring home several hunks if they are vacuum sealed. Available online, it's often hard to find in local markets. That's why we often recommend the easy-to-find pecorino Romano, flintier, saltier, and easy to grate. Parmigiano Reggiano suits this recipe, too.

# Cavatappi with Pancetta, Artichokes, Tomatoes, and Olives

SERVES 4 TO 6

In a large pot of boiling salted water, cook the cavatappi until al dente, about 9 minutes. Do not drain.

Meanwhile, in a large skillet, cook the pancetta in the olive oil over medium-high heat for 1 minute. Add the onion and cook, stirring often, until the onion is softened and the pancetta has rendered most of its fat, about 2 minutes. Add the tomatoes and roll them around to heat through, about 2 minutes. Scoop out ½ cup (120 ml) of the pasta water and add it to the pan along with the artichokes, olives, fennel seeds, and oregano. Season with salt and pepper. Reduce the heat to low and simmer for 3 minutes.

When the cavatappi is al dente, scoop out another ½ cup (120 ml) of the pasta water before draining. Add the pasta to the pan and toss with the artichoke mixture, moistening with the extra pasta water, if needed. Serve in bowls and top with the cheese.

12 ounces (340 g) cavatappi

3½ ounces (100 g) diced pancetta

3 tablespoons extra-virgin olive oil

1 onion, finely chopped

16 cherry tomatoes, halved

1 (1-pound/455 g) jar marinated artichoke hearts, drained

½ cup (80 g) pitted and halved green olives, such as Castelvetrano

1 teaspoon fennel seeds

½ teaspoon dried oregano

Coarse salt and freshly ground black pepper

Grated pecorino Romano

**Italy is the wonderland** of *salume*, none more adored than spicy mortadella. Banish all thoughts of lunchroom bologna sandwiches! *Mortadella* (of the mortar) is finely ground pork with at least 15 percent fat, often flavored with myrtle berries or allspice, garlic, pistachios, crushed peppercorns, chopped olives, or even caraway seeds. This redolent meat adds vivid flavor, and the pistachios provide a crunch.

# Cavatelli with Mortadella, Ricotta, and Cherry Tomatoes

SERVES 4 TO 6

12 ounces (340 g) cavatelli

2 cloves garlic, minced

¼ cup (60 ml) extra-virgin olive oil

20 cherry tomatoes, a mix of red and yellow, halved

1 cup (8 ounces/250 g) whole-milk ricotta

1 teaspoon crushed black pepper

Coarse salt

8 ounces (225 g) mortadella, cubed

3 tablespoons chopped pistachios

Grated pecorino Romano

In a large pot of boiling salted water, cook the cavatelli until al dente, about 9 minutes; drain.

In a large skillet, cook the garlic in the olive oil over medium heat until fragrant, 1 to 2 minutes. Add the tomatoes and cook, stirring, until they begin to soften, about 3 minutes. Mix in the ricotta, crushed pepper, and salt. Reduce the heat to low, cover, and simmer for 3 minutes.

Add the mortadella and pistachios and heat through. Add the cooked pasta and toss to mix well. Serve in bowls and pass the cheese on the side.

In restaurants all over Puglia, you see this pasta, the favorite of the region, being made at astonishing speed, usually by a skilled woman seated at a table near the kitchen. She forms the pasta dough into "little ears," perfectly shaped to cup the many local sauces made from bitter greens. Way south in the heel of the boot of Italy, seafood reigns, but Puglia grows much of Italy's produce ,and the local cuisine relishes its greens.

# Orecchiette with Pancetta, Broccoli Rabe, Burrata, and Pine Nuts

SERVES 6

12 ounces (340 g) orecchiette

1 bunch broccoli rabe (about 12 ounces/340 g)

8 ounces (225 g) cubed pancetta (about 1½ cups)

3 tablespoons extra-virgin olive oil

7½ ounces (215 g) burrata, mashed into small pieces

Coarse salt and freshly ground black pepper

½ cup (50 g) grated Parmigiano Reggiano

¼ cup (35 g) toasted pine nuts

In a large pot of boiling salted water, cook the orecchiette until al dente, 15 to 18 minutes. Reserve 1 cup (240 ml) of the pasta water before draining.

Steam the broccoli rabe until just tender but still bright green, 3 to 5 minutes. Rinse briefly under cold running water. Drain and chop very coarsely.

In a large skillet, fry the pancetta in the olive oil over medium-high heat, stirring, until browned and crispy, about 3 minutes. Add the broccoli rabe to the pan, then the burrata. Use tongs to distribute the greens, which tend to clump. Season with salt and pepper.

Add the cooked pasta and half of the reserved water to the skillet. Toss to mix well. In a small bowl, stir the buratta and half of the Parmigiano into the remaining reserved pasta water until creamy. Pour over the pasta, add 3 tablespoons of the pine nuts, and toss again. Transfer to a serving bowl and sprinkle the remaining pine nuts and Parmigiano on top.

The spicy salami really tweaks this hearty pasta that's as perfect on a cold night as it is for a summer picnic. In Italy, what we know as lacinato, or dinosaur, kale is called *cavolo nero* (black cabbage). It's one of the most nutritious of vegetables, and when not overcooked, is surprisingly delicate and delicious. Serve with a generous sprinkling of pecorino Romano. Medium-size *conchiglie* (shells) are also a good pasta option.

# Penne with Pepperoni, Kale, Chickpeas, and Sweet Peppers

SERVES 4

In a large pot of boiling salted water, cook the penne over high heat until just al dente, about 10 minutes. Reserve 1 cup (240 ml) of the pasta water before draining.

Meanwhile, in a large skillet, heat 3 tablespoons of the olive oil over medium-high heat. Add the garlic and sauté for 30 seconds, then add the bell pepper and hot pepper. Sauté until the bell pepper is just softened, about 2 minutes. Add the kale and salt and sauté for 1 minute, to wilt slightly. Reduce the heat to medium, add the chickpeas and pepperoni, cover, and cook until the kale is tender but still bright green, 2 to 3 minutes.

Add the pasta and reserved pasta water and simmer until the pasta has absorbed most of the liquid, about 2 minutes. Remove from the heat and toss with the pecorino. Serve with additional grated cheese on the side.

8 ounces (225 g) penne rigate

¼ cup (60 ml) extra-virgin olive oil

3 cloves garlic, thinly sliced

1 red or yellow bell pepper, thinly sliced, or use ½ red and ½ yellow

¾ teaspoon crushed hot red pepper

1 small bunch lacinato kale (about 8 ounces/225 g), stemmed and cut into thick ribbons

¾ teaspoon coarse salt

1 (15-ounce/425 g) can chickpeas, rinsed and drained

2 ounces (55 g) thinly sliced pepperoni, slivered

⅓ cup (35 g) grated pecorino Romano, plus more for the table

We like pairing sedanini, or "little celery stalks," with its namesake. Fresh celery, prosciutto, plus crusty breadcrumbs spiked with lemon—these tasty ingredients lend texture to this opening salvo to dinner. Beware of adding too much salt, as the prosciutto and pasta water are salty. If the celery has pretty leaves, clip some for garnish. Other pastas to consider: pipe rigate and penne.

# Sedanini with Prosciutto, Celery, and Lemon-Scented Breadcrumbs

SERVES 4 TO 6

12 ounces (340 g) sedanini

5 tablespoons (75 ml) extra-virgin olive oil

¾ cup (75 g) coarse breadcrumbs

Grated zest of 1 lemon, plus 2 tablespoons juice

Coarse salt and freshly ground black pepper

1 cup (100 g) diced celery, plus a few celery leaves for garnish

5 ounces (140 g) prosciutto, cut into 1-inch-wide (2.5 cm) strips

¼ cup (60 ml) dry white wine

2 ounces (55 g) Fontina cheese, finely diced (about ½ cup)

1 teaspoon fresh oregano, or ½ teaspoon dried

½ teaspoon minced fresh rosemary

In a large pot of boiling salted water, cook the sedanini until al dente, 9 to 10 minutes. Reserve ½ cup (120 ml) of the pasta water before draining.

Meanwhile, in a large skillet, heat 2 tablespoons of the olive oil. Toss in the breadcrumbs and cook, stirring, over medium-high heat until they are lightly browned, about 2 minutes. Sprinkle on the lemon zest and season with a little salt and pepper. Remove the breadcrumbs to a plate and wipe out any remaining bits in the skillet.

Add the remaining 3 tablespoons olive oil to the skillet. Add the celery and cook over medium heat, stirring occasionally, until softened but still slightly crunchy, about 3 minutes. Toss in the prosciutto and cook, stirring, for 1 minute. Pour in the wine and bring to a boil. Reduce the heat to low.

Pour the reserved pasta water into the skillet. Add the Fontina, lemon juice, oregano, rosemary, and pepper to taste. Cover and cook, stirring often, for 2 minutes, or until the Fontina melts. Add the pasta and toss to mix. Transfer to a large serving bowl, sprinkle the breadcrumbs on top, and garnish with the celery leaves, if using.

Here's a recipe that uses rotisserie chicken, or leftover cooked chicken, to great advantage (see also page 191). Because the ingredients are rich, as a main course it's best accompanied by simple vegetables, such as braised carrots with ginger, lightly splashed with balsamic vinegar, and green beans steamed with shallots with a squeeze of lemon juice.

# Fusilli with Chicken Marsala and Mushrooms

SERVES 4

In a large pot of boiling salted water, cook the fusilli until al dente, 10 to 11 minutes; drain.

Meanwhile, in a large skillet, melt the butter in the olive oil. Add the shallot and then the mushrooms. Sauté over high heat, stirring and tossing occasionally, until the mushrooms begin to give up their juices and are lightly browned, about 3 minutes.

Pour in the Marsala and let it bubble for a few seconds, then add the chicken broth, cream, and tarragon. Bring to a boil, reduce the heat to medium, and simmer for 3 minutes to blend the flavors and reduce the sauce slightly. Stir in the lemon juice and season generously with salt and pepper. Add the chicken to the sauce and simmer, stirring occasionally, for 5 minutes.

To serve, mound the cooked fusilli in a large serving bowl. Pour the sauce over the pasta and toss to mix well.

12 ounces (340 g) fusilli

2 tablespoons unsalted butter

2 tablespoons extra-virgin olive oil

1 shallot, thinly sliced

8 ounces (225 g) white button or baby bella (cremini) mushrooms, sliced

⅓ cup (80 ml) Marsala wine or medium-dry sherry

1½ cups (360 ml) chicken broth

⅔ cup (160 ml) heavy cream

1 teaspoon dried tarragon

1 tablespoon fresh lemon juice

Coarse salt and freshly ground black pepper

12 ounces (340 g) rotisserie chicken or leftover roast chicken, coarsely shredded (about 2 cups)

Italian sausage labeled "sweet" often has a more complex flavor than the hot variety. The other spices, such as fennel, are more pronounced, and the heat can always be enhanced by adding hot pepper. The large, medium, or small *conchiglie* (snails or seashells) are designed to trap sauce, and they succeed. Their pleasing shape guarantees an attractive presentation. This is a robust pasta that reheats with even more intensity.

# Conchiglie with Italian Sausage, Kale, and Sun-Dried Tomatoes

SERVES 4

10 ounces (280 g) medium conchiglie

¼ cup (60 ml) extra-virgin olive oil

4 or 5 cloves garlic, halved lengthwise, then sliced

½ teaspoon crushed hot red pepper

10 ounces sweet or spicy Italian sausage, casing removed

1 large bunch kale (10 to 12 ounces/280 to 340 g), stems removed, leaves torn into 2-inch (5 cm) pieces

½ cup (40 g) oil-packed sun-dried tomato strips

Coarse salt and freshly ground black pepper

Grated Parmigiano Reggiano (optional)

In a large pot of boiling salted water, cook the pasta until al dente, 10 to 11 minutes. Reserve 1 cup (240 ml) of the pasta water before draining.

In a large deep skillet, heat the olive oil. Add the garlic and hot pepper and sauté over medium-high heat, stirring often, until the garlic is soft and fragrant, about 1 minute. Crumble the sausage into the skillet. Cook, breaking up the meat as much as possible, until it is lightly browned and no longer pink, 4 to 5 minutes.

Add the kale to the skillet along with ⅓ cup (80 ml) plain water. Stir to mix with the sausage and garlicky oil. Cover, reduce the heat to medium, and cook, stirring once or twice, until the kale is tender but still bright green, about 3 minutes.

Add the pasta to the skillet along with the reserved pasta water. Stir in the sun-dried tomatoes and season with salt and pepper. Simmer, tossing, for about 2 minutes to blend the flavors. Pass the cheese, if desired, with the bowls of pasta.

**Michelin-star chef Silvia Baracchi** owns the sybaritic country inn Il Falconieri and restaurant just outside Cortona. Located in the middle of her vineyard, the inn is a magnet for those seeking creative food with deep Tuscan roots and also the joyous experience of dining in an environment imbued with old-world luxury. Guests love her Cooking Under the Tuscan Sun Cooking School. Recently, she was teaching us how to make this rustic but sophisticated pasta cooked in a whole bottle of red wine, which turns it a dark, intriguing burgundy color. *Calamarata* pasta (shown in the photograph), named for its resemblance to sliced calamari, is Silvia's choice for this pasta. We also recommend the easy-to-find cavatappi.

# Silvia Baracchi's Red Wine Cavatappi with Sausage and Sautéed Onions

SERVES 4 TO 6

In a large stainless-steel pot, bring 6½ cups (1.5 liters) water, red wine, bay leaf, thyme, sugar, and 1 tablespoon of the salt to a boil. Add the cavatappi and cook, stirring once or twice, until al dente, about 10 minutes. Reserve ¼ cup (60 ml) of the wine broth before draining the pasta.

Meanwhile, in a large skillet, sauté the onions in 3 tablespoons of the olive oil over high heat, stirring often, until softened and golden, about 3 minutes. Add the garlic and hot pepper and cook for 1 minute longer. Remove to a bowl and cover to keep warm.

Add the remaining 2 tablespoons olive oil and the sausage to the skillet and cook over high heat, stirring to break up the meat with a large spoon, until it is lightly browned, 3 to 4 minutes. Pour in the white wine and bring to a boil. Reduce the heat to medium and cook until the wine almost evaporates, about 2 minutes. Season with the thyme, pepper, and remaining ¼ teaspoon salt. Reduce the heat to low.

As soon as the pasta is al dente, add it to the sausage along with the reserved red wine broth. Toss well and simmer for a couple minutes to blend the flavors.

To serve, divide the onions among individual plates, spreading them into a thin layer. Arrange the pasta then the sausage on top. Garnish with the parsley and chives. Sprinkle with the cheese and garnish with flowers, parsley, or chives, if using.

1 (750-ml) bottle full-bodied red wine

1 bay leaf

1 teaspoon fresh thyme

1 tablespoon sugar

1¼ tablespoons coarse salt

12 ounces (340 g) cavatappi

2 onions, thinly sliced

5 tablespoons (75 ml) extra-virgin olive oil

2 cloves garlic, finely chopped

¼ teaspoon crushed hot red pepper

3 Italian sweet sausages (4 ounces/115 g each), casing removed

¾ cup (180 ml) dry white wine

1 teaspoon fresh thyme

¼ teaspoon freshly ground black pepper

½ cup shredded pecorino Romano

Optional garnishes: edible flowers, chopped flat-leaf parsley, minced fresh chives

*Casarecce* means home cooking, which this warm-hearted recipe exemplifies. When Prometheus stole fire from the gods, he brought coals to mankind inside a fennel bulb. At our house Bramasole, we gather the umbrella-shaped yellow flowers at the end of summer, shaking the pollen into a bag, then drying the blossoms outdoors on screens. These are also flavorful. Every bit of the cultivated fennel is useful, from the knobby white bulb to feathery fronds that enhance salads and make pretty garnishes. Any flowers gone to seed are grabbed—fennel seeds define Italian *finocchiona* sausages, pork roasts, rabbit, and game. Then there's *finocchietto*, a strong elixir like limoncello, only made with fennel.

# Casarecce with Sausage, Cannellini Beans, Chard, and Fennel Pollen

**SERVES 4 TO 6**

12 ounces (340 g) casarecce

2 tablespoons extra-virgin olive oil

1 pound (450 g) Italian sweet sausage, casing removed

2 cloves garlic, minced

1 bunch Swiss chard (about 1 pound/450 g), stems removed, leaves slivered (about 3 cups)

1 (14-ounce/400 g) can cannellini beans, rinsed and drained

¼ teaspoon fennel pollen

¼ teaspoon crushed hot red pepper

Coarse salt and freshly ground black pepper

Grated pecorino Romano

In a large pot of boiling salted water, cook the casarecce until al dente, about 10 minutes. Reserve 1 cup (240 ml) of the pasta water before draining.

Meanwhile, add the olive oil to a large deep skillet set over medium-high heat. Crumble the sausage into the pan and add the garlic. Cook, stirring to break up the sausage, until the meat is lightly browned and no longer pink, about 4 minutes.

While the sausage is browning, steam the chard until tender, 3 to 4 minutes. Drain and add to the sausage, along with the cannellini beans, fennel pollen, and hot pepper. Mix well.

Add the casarecce and ½ cup (120 ml) of the reserved pasta water to the skillet. Toss over medium-high heat, adding more of the reserved water if needed to moisten. Season with salt and pepper to taste. Toss and serve in individual bowls. Pass the cheese.

If you go to Italy, you may be bringing home treats such as fennel pollen, cubes of fungi porcini broth, Domori chocolate, pecorino cheese, and special pastas. Save room for *pignoli*, Italian-grown pine nuts, as well. Most of them sold in the United States come from China and are expensive, but in Italy they're fresh, affordable, and also will remind you of the sculptural pines that punctuate the landscape. Vacuum packed, they're legal to import. Fusilli comes in different sizes so check the cooking time on the package.

# Fusilli with Sausage, Sun-Dried Tomatoes, Spinach, and Pine Nuts

SERVES 4

In a large pot of boiling salted water, cook the fusilli until al dente, 9 to 10 minutes. Reserve 1 cup (240 ml) of the pasta water before draining.

Meanwhile, add the olive oil to a large skillet set over medium-high heat. Crumble the sausage into the pan and cook, stirring to break up the sausage, until the meat is lightly browned and no longer pink, about 4 minutes. Add the garlic, sun-dried tomatoes, spinach, oregano, and a pinch of salt. Mix well and continue to cook over low heat for 3 to 4 minutes.

Add the cooked fusilli and ½ cup (120 ml) of the reserved water to the skillet. Raise the heat to medium-high and cook, stirring, for 2 to 3 minutes, adding more of the pasta water if needed to moisten. Stir in the pine nuts. Serve in bowls, topped with the cheese.

12 ounces (340 g) fusilli

3 tablespoons extra-virgin olive oil

1 pound (450 g) Italian sausage, sweet or spicy, casing removed

3 cloves garlic, minced

½ cup (55 g) chopped oil-packed sun-dried tomatoes

1 cup (155 g) chopped frozen spinach, thawed

½ teaspoon dried oregano

Coarse salt

¼ cup (30 g) toasted pine nuts

½ cup (50 g) grated Parmigiano Reggiano

*Paglia e fieno,* straw and hay, is golden and green, the "straw" pasta containing eggs and the "hay" pasta incorporating spinach. Find them separately or packaged together. This is a traditional Sunday pasta of the Siena area. Rich with cream and utterly simple, it's a down-home food of memory for many. Sliced baked ham or speck can be substituted for the prosciutto.

# Straw and Hay Tagliatelle with Prosciutto and Peas

SERVES 4 TO 6

6 ounces (170 g) tagliatelle made with eggs

6 ounces (170 g) tagliatelle made with spinach

3 tablespoons unsalted butter

6 plump scallions, thinly sliced

1 cup (145 g) peas, fresh or thawed frozen

¾ cup (180 ml) heavy cream

4 ounces (145 g) prosciutto, cut lengthwise into thin strips

2 tablespoons coarsely chopped black olives

¼ teaspoon freshly grated nutmeg

4 or 5 fresh sage leaves, slivered

Coarse salt and freshly ground black pepper

¾ cup (75 g) grated Parmigiano Reggiano or Grana Padano

In a large pot of boiling salted water, cook the tagliatelle until al dente, stirring once or twice to mix the colors, about 9 minutes.

Meanwhile, in a large skillet, melt the butter over medium heat. Add the scallions and cook, stirring until softened, 1 to 2 minutes. Add the peas and cook for 2 minutes. Pour in the cream, add the prosciutto and olives, and season with the nutmeg and sage. Bring to a simmer, then cook over low heat for 2 to 3 minutes, stirring a few times. Season with salt and pepper. Stir in half the cheese.

When the pasta is al dente, transfer it with tongs directly into the sauce and toss well. Serve in bowls, topped with the rest of the cheese.

This quick version of the quintessential long-simmered Italian meat sauce is a last-minute time saver. Nothing beats traditional Tuscan ragù, simmered for hours, perfuming the kitchen with the promise of the robust pasta everyone loves. Here, we foreground the taste and cut the time. High heat, sun-dried tomatoes, amped-up herbs, plenty of garlic, and red wine all lend intensity. Two skillets speed up the process. Add a great salad, garlic-rubbed bruschetta—and you're done. Leftover sauce over bruschetta is a great lunch. Ragù freezes well for up to 5 months and easily keeps in the fridge for 5 days. *Stracci*, rags, are easily available online and are so useful to have on hand. They're rough squares, up to 4 by 4 inches (10 by 10 cm) that can be cut or torn from a sheet of fresh pasta, broken from dry lasagna sheets, or improvised from leftover pasta dough. If you don't have stracci, spaghetti always loves ragù! Parmigiano is classic but this dish is also good with cubes of mozzarella, as shown here.

# Stracci with Almost-Instant Ragù

SERVES 6

In a large pot of boiling salted water, cook the stracci until al dente, 9 to 10 minutes; drain.

Meanwhile, in a medium saucepan, heat 3 tablespoons of the olive oil. Add the onion and garlic and sauté over high heat, stirring, until the onion softens, about 2 minutes. Stir in the sun-dried and chopped tomatoes, oregano, and thyme. Bring to a boil, reduce the heat to low, and simmer the tomato sauce, stirring occasionally, while you prepare the meat.

In a large skillet, heat the remaining 2 tablespoons olive oil. Crumble the beef and sausage into the pan and sauté over high heat, stirring to break up the meat, until it is no longer pink, about 5 minutes. Add the red wine, bring to a boil, and boil for 2 minutes to reduce slightly. Add the tomato sauce and basil, reduce the heat to medium-low, cover, and simmer for 3 minutes to blend the flavors. Season with salt and pepper to taste. (Makes about 5 cups.)

Arrange the stracci on a large platter and top with ladles of ragù and a big sprinkle of Parmigiano. Garnish with basil sprigs.

1 pound (450 g) stracci

5 tablespoons (75 ml) extra-virgin olive oil

1 onion, finely chopped

4 cloves garlic, minced

3 tablespoons finely chopped oil-packed sun-dried tomatoes

1 (14½-ounce/410 g) can chopped tomatoes

½ teaspoon dried oregano, or 1 teaspoon fresh

½ teaspoon dried thyme, or 1 teaspoon fresh

8 ounces (225 g) lean ground beef

8 ounces (225 g) sweet Italian sausage, casing removed

¾ cup (180 ml) full-bodied red wine

10 fresh basil leaves, torn, plus a few sprigs for garnish

Coarse salt and freshly ground black pepper

Grated Parmigiano Reggiano

A favorite on the menu at the neighborhood restaurant Parione in Florence is the filet mignon in caramelized onions. Our recipe is a pasta adaption of the idea. This is an extravagant party-night special. Start the dinner with a crisp green vegetable—asparagus with lemon or sautéed zucchini with tomatoes and basil—and this pasta takes you all the way to dessert. Use two skillets, as the steak cooks in a flash and is added at the last moment. Balsamic vinegar is a crucial ingredient—quality counts. Best to select a bottle that specifies it's from Modena or Reggio Emilia and the only ingredient is grape must. The longer it was aged, the higher the price. Those labeled *Condimento* may be fine but were made outside the designated zone. Often, not always, they are cheaper. Many supermarket balsamics and condimentos have added caramel flavoring, which is simply not the same thing as balsamic. For cooking, balsamic vinegar should be added toward the end, as heat destroys its sweet, leathery flavors.

# Spaghetti with Filet Mignon and Herbed Balsamic Onions

SERVES 6

1 pound (450 g) spaghetti

6 tablespoons (90 ml) extra-virgin olive oil

3 red onions, thinly sliced

Coarse salt

⅓ cup (80 ml) balsamic vinegar

½ teaspoon dried thyme, or 1 teaspoon fresh

Freshly ground black pepper

⅓ cup (80 ml) dry red wine

1 pound (450 g) filet mignon, cut against the grain into ¼-inch-thick (6 mm) slices, then quartered into 2-inch (5 cm) pieces

1 teaspoon chopped fresh rosemary, plus sprigs for garnish

½ ounce (14 g) dried porcini mushrooms

In a large pot of salted boiling water, cook the spaghetti until just al dente, 9 to 10 minutes. Reserve ½ cup (120 ml) of the pasta water before draining.

Meanwhile, in a large deep skillet, heat 3 tablespoons of the olive oil. Add the onions and ½ teaspoon salt. Sauté over high heat, stirring often, until softened and beginning to color, 3 to 4 minutes. Add the balsamic vinegar, thyme, and a grind of pepper. Reduce the heat to medium-low and cook, stirring often, until the onions are soft and richly dark, about 3 minutes. Crank up the heat, add the red wine, and let it come to a boil boil, then remove from the heat and cover to keep warm.

While the onions cook, toss the steak pieces with 1 tablespoon olive oil, the chopped rosemary, and several grinds of pepper. Set aside.

Crumble the dried mushrooms into a small heatproof glass bowl, add 1 cup (240 ml) water, and microwave on high for 2 minutes. Add the mushrooms to the skillet, along with 3 tablespoons of their cooking water. Mix well.

Add the spaghetti and reserved pasta water to the balsamic onions. Toss to mix well. Set over low heat while you sear the steak.

Heat the remaining 2 tablespoons olive oil in a large heavy skillet until almost smoking. Add the steak pieces and sear, tossing over high heat, for just 20 to 30 seconds, so the meat remains pink. Watch, as it is so easy to overcook. (If you prefer well done, allow up to 1 minute.) Quickly remove from the heat and toss half the steak with the pasta. Divide among individual bowls, arrange the rest of the steak on top, and garnish with sprigs of rosemary.

This is a big hit, easy for a family supper and just as special for dinner with friends. Curly-edged malfadine adds to the fun but any flat pasta will work. Veal cooks quickly, so keep an eye on it. No Marsala? Use a dry white wine.

# Malfadine with Veal Strips, Mushrooms, and Preserved Lemon

SERVES 4

In a large pot of boiling salted water, cook the pasta until al dente, 10 to 12 minutes. Reserve ½ cup (120 ml) of the pasta water before draining.

Meanwhile, in a large heavy skillet, heat 3 tablespoons of the olive oil. Add the shallots and bay leaf, then the mushrooms and thyme. Sauté over high heat, stirring often, until the mushrooms are lightly browned, about 4 minutes. Add the Marsala and boil for a few seconds. Reduce the heat to low and stir in the lemon. Keep warm over the lowest heat.

In another large heavy skillet, heat the remaining 2 tablespoons olive oil. When very hot, toss in the veal strips and sauté over medium-high heat, flipping to brown the outside and cook the meat, about 1 minute. Lightly season with salt and pepper.

Add the pasta to the mushrooms, and toss to mix well, adding as much of the reserved pasta water as needed to moisten. Serve in shallow bowls with the veal strips on top. Garnish with chopped chives and rosemary.

12 ounces (340 g) malfadine

5 tablespoons (75 ml) extra-virgin olive oil

2 shallots, minced

1 bay leaf

1 pound (450 g) baby bella (cremini) mushrooms, sliced

1 teaspoon fresh thyme, or ½ teaspoon dried

¼ cup (60 ml) Marsala wine

1 tablespoon chopped preserved lemon, or grated zest and juice of 1 lemon

12 ounces (340 g) veal scallopini, about ¼ inch (6 mm) thick, cut into ½-inch-wide (12 mm) strips

Coarse salt and freshly ground black pepper

Chopped chives and rosemary sprigs, for garnish

Juicy lean lamb, cooked just until pink, is paired here with the sweetness of red peppers and pleasing tang of salty olives, all enlivened with rosemary, thyme, and a hit of hot pepper for a distinctly Mediterranean pasta elegant enough for a dinner party. There is so much flavor, no cheese is needed, but a glistening last-minute spritz of extra-virgin olive oil is recommended. If you can't imagine pasta without cheese, opt for pecorino. As a main course, serve with sides of steamed Broccolini or green beans, dressed with lemon juice and olive oil.

# Penne Rigate with Lamb, Roasted Red Peppers, and Olives

**SERVES 4**

8 ounces (225 g) lamb tenderloin or steak from the leg, cut into 1½ by ¼-inch (4 cm by 6 mm) strips

2 teaspoons chopped fresh rosemary, or 1 teaspoon dried

1 teaspoon dried thyme

¼ teaspoon crushed hot red pepper

3 tablespoons plus 1 teaspoon extra-virgin olive oil

Coarse salt and freshly ground black pepper

8 ounces (225 g) penne rigate

½ onion, thinly sliced

2 cloves garlic, thinly sliced

2 plum tomatoes, diced

¾ cup (70 g) roasted red pepper strips

½ cup (90 g) pitted Kalamata or Gaeta olives

Chopped fresh flat-leaf parsley

In a small bowl, toss the lamb with half the rosemary, the thyme, hot pepper, and 1 teaspoon of the olive oil. Season lightly with salt and generously with freshly ground black pepper. Set aside.

In a large pot of boiling salted water, cook the penne until al dente, 9 to 11 minutes. Reserve ½ cup (120 ml) of the pasta water before draining.

Meanwhile, set a large heavy skillet, preferably cast-iron, over high heat. Add the remaining 3 tablespoons olive oil and heat for 30 seconds. Add the onion and garlic and sauté, stirring often, until the onion is beginning to color, 2 to 3 minutes. Toss in the lamb and sear, stirring once, for 30 seconds. Add the tomatoes and sauté for 2 minutes, or until they just soften. Reduce the heat to medium-low. Add the roasted peppers and olives. Simmer for 1 minute to blend the flavors. Stir in the reserved pasta water.

Add the cooked pasta to the skillet. Toss to mix and coat with the sauce. Warm through for a minute, then divide among four plates. Garnish with chopped parsley.

While you can also use any leftover chicken you have on hand, this is best made with rotisserie chicken because its super-moist texture soaks up all the juices in the sauce. The potent tomato sauce with peppers and onions is reminiscent of Italian-American chicken cacciatore.

# Rigatoni with Fiery Rosemary Chicken, Peppers, and Onions

SERVES 4

In a large pot of boiling salted water, cook the pasta until al dente, 12 to 14 minutes.

Meanwhile, in a large heavy skillet, warm 3 tablespoons of the olive oil over high heat until almost smoking. Add the onion and sauté, tossing, for 1 to 2 minutes, until beginning to soften and color around the edges. Add the peppers and sauté, tossing often, for about 2 minutes, until they just begin to soften but still maintain their bright color. Transfer to a bowl.

Add the remaining 2 tablespoons oil to the skillet and reduce the heat to medium. Add the garlic, hot pepper, and anchovy paste. Cook until the garlic just begins to color, about 2 minutes. Add the tomato paste and cook, stirring, for 1 minute, or until it starts to darken. Pour in the passata, add ¾ cup (180 ml) water, and season with the rosemary, salt, and sugar. Simmer the sauce over medium-low heat for 2 to 3 minutes.

Add the sautéed onion and peppers and the chicken to the sauce and simmer for 2 minutes. If the pasta is not done yet, turn off the heat and let the sauce sit to maintain a bit of crunch in the vegetables. If it becomes too thick, thin with a little more water.

As soon as the pasta is just tender, drain and add it to the sauce. Simmer for a minute or two and serve.

8 ounces (225 g) rigatoni

5 tablespoons (75 ml) extra-virgin olive oil

1 onion, thinly sliced

1 large red bell pepper, cut into thin slices

1 small green bell pepper, cut into thin slices

2 cloves garlic, chopped

½ to 1 teaspoon crushed hot red pepper, to taste

1 teaspoon anchovy paste

1½ tablespoons tomato paste

1½ cups (355 ml) passata

1 tablespoon minced fresh rosemary

1 teaspoon coarse salt

Pinch of sugar

8 to 10 ounces (225 to 280 g) rotisserie chicken or leftover roast chicken (1½ to 2 cups), torn into large shreds

When you buy duck confit, it is fully cooked, which makes it perfect for a *veloce* pasta. Vacuum-packed cooked, peeled chestnuts are also readily available. In Tuscany, nothing is more magical than gathering chestnuts on a sunny autumn afternoon when the leaves of the old-growth trees are blazing yellow and the sun falls in shafts through the branches. Once at home, you're faced with opening the spiny shells that look like tiny porcupines. Inside, the chestnut is again protected by its smooth and shiny shell. Not so fun to extract the nut, but worth the trouble. Almost every Tuscan family has a long-handled, pierced metal chestnut roaster. Ed's fireside skills are splitting the shells so they peel open once roasted—and pouring a glass of Barolo to go with them. This unusual recipe will be the highlight of the fall holidays. Susan's unconventional reduction of coffee and balsamic vinegar, along with a splash of soy, creates a lush, rich sauce with caramel overtones. For best flavor, use a medium rather than dark roast coffee.

# Tagliatelle with Duck Confit and Chestnuts

SERVES 4

8 ounces (225 g) tagliatelle

½ cup (120 ml) medium roast brewed coffee

1½ tablespoons balsamic vinegar

1 teaspoon soy sauce

½ teaspoon turbinado or light brown sugar

½ teaspoon fresh thyme leaves, or ¼ teaspoon dried

3 tablespoons unsalted butter

Coarse salt and freshly ground black pepper

2 duck confit legs (about 5 ounces/140 g each), coarsely shredded, skin and fat removed

6½ to 7 ounces (about 200 g) cooked peeled chestnuts

Sprigs of fresh thyme or chopped fresh flat-leaf parsley

In a large pot of boiling salted water, cook the tagliatelle until just barely al dente, 4 to 5 minutes. Reserve ½ cup (120 ml) of the pasta water.

Meanwhile, in a large skillet, combine the coffee, balsamic vinegar, soy sauce, sugar, and thyme. Bring to a boil over medium-high heat and continue to cook until the liquid is reduced slightly, about 3 minutes. Whisk in the butter, 1 tablespoon at a time. Season with salt and pepper to taste. Add the duck and chestnuts to the sauce and simmer for 1 to 2 minutes to heat through.

Using tongs, transfer the pasta along with the water that clings to it to the sauce. Toss to mix. Simmer for another minute. If the dish seems too dry, add ¼ to ½ cup (60 to 120 ml) of the pasta water. Serve at once, garnished with thyme sprigs or chopped parsley.

The Romans eat well, and as we see in the photograph, certainly know how to relax in their piazzas. *Saltimbocca* means "jump in the mouth," and this pasta version does just that. The traditional Roman saltimbocca is an entrée made with veal scallopini. In this riff, ground turkey is paired with the distinctive saltimbocca ingredients: sage and prosciutto. Use a good white wine in the sauce and enjoy the rest with dinner.

# Rigatoni with Turkey Saltimbocca

SERVES 4

12 ounces (340 g) rigatoni

¼ cup (60 ml) extra-virgin olive oil

2 ounces (60 g) prosciutto, cut into thin strips

1 onion, thinly sliced

½ teaspoon coarse salt

2 tablespoons finely shredded fresh sage

1 pound (450 g) ground turkey

¼ teaspoon freshly grated nutmeg

¼ teaspoon freshly ground black pepper

½ cup (120 ml) dry white wine

⅔ cup (160 ml) chicken stock

2 tablespoons unsalted butter

In a large pot of boiling salted water, cook the rigatoni until the pasta is al dente, about 12 minutes.

Meanwhile, in a very large skillet, heat 3 tablespoons of the oil. Add the prosciutto and cook over medium heat, stirring to separate the strands, for about 2 minutes, until most of the fat is rendered but before the meat crisps. Remove the prosciutto to a plate, pressing against the side of the pan to leave as much oil behind as possible.

Add the remaining 1 tablespoon oil and the onion slices to the pan. Sprinkle on the salt. Cook over high heat, stirring often, for 2 minutes. Add the sage and continue to cook until the onion softens and begins to color around the edges, about 2 minutes longer.

Add the turkey to the pan and reduce the heat to medium-high. Season with the nutmeg and pepper and sauté, breaking up the turkey into small clumps, until it is no longer pink and some pieces are lightly browned, 4 to 5 minutes. Pour in the wine and boil for 1 minute to reduce slightly. Add the chicken stock and simmer for another 2 minutes. Stir in the butter until just melted. Season with additional salt and pepper to taste.

When the pasta is al dente, drain and turn into a large serving bowl. Pour the turkey saltimbocca sauce on top, toss, and serve.

# Pestos

Pesto comes from "pestle," hearkening to the early and effective method of using a mortar and pestle, usually stone or marble in Italy, to smash together aromatic ingredients and often nuts, which, with the addition of olive oil, creates an emulsion and produces an intensely flavored thick sauce, usually used for pasta. Some pasta water is often blended in shortly before serving to achieve a nice coating consistency. The most famous pesto from Liguria (page 200) combines copious amounts of fresh basil leaves with pine nuts, garlic, and olive oil. Other pestos can be based on a vegetable, such as kale or arugula, or a creamy cheese, such as fresh white goat cheese, for a mellower sauce.

The pestos featured here have many talents other than for pasta sauces. For example, dab a little basil pesto on pizza or baked tomatoes stuffed with rice, on grilled chicken, in vegetable soups, or spread it on bruschetta. Check individual recipes for their particular suggested uses. Pesto is best left with a bit of texture, rather than a completely smooth puree. There's nothing handier than a pesto in the fridge—grab it for crackers, crostini, vegetable dips, and pastas for an instant treat. The pestos can be doubled, with the exception of the Walnut Pesto (page 211). Freeze serving sizes in jars, ice cube trays, or plastic bags.

Aromatic and lustrous Genovese basil grows easily in partial shade, often turning into a knee-high bush. Even the little pots for sale in the supermarket will thrive if repotted and left in a partly sunny window. Basil pesto, a summer-night staple with spaghetti, seems to be loved by everyone. Before serving, toss in some blistered cherry tomatoes if you want.

# Classic Basil Pesto

MAKES ABOUT 1¾ CUPS (420 ML)

4 cups (80 g) lightly packed fresh basil leaves

¼ cup (60 g) pine nuts

3 cloves garlic, quartered

¼ teaspoon coarse salt

¾ cup (180 ml) extra-virgin olive oil

½ cup (50 g) grated Parmigiano Reggiano

In a food processor or blender, combine the basil, pine nuts, garlic, and salt. Pulse about 8 times, until coarsely chopped. With the machine on, slowly pour in the olive oil, stopping as soon as it is absorbed.

When the pesto is an emerald-green puree, add the Parmigiano and pulse another 8 or 9 times to mix it in.

This is a thick, creamy pesto that's superb as a pasta sauce. When tossing with the pasta, you may want to thin it with a little of the pasta water. This recipe makes enough pesto to sauce 8 to 10 ounces (225 to 280 g) of pasta. It keeps well for up to three days. If you omit the pasta water, this makes a fine spread for crostini or a dip for raw vegetables.

# Goat Cheese and Walnut Pesto

MAKES ABOUT 2 CUPS (480 ML)

Heat the olive oil in a heavy, very small saucepan. Add the garlic and cook over the lowest heat for 3 minutes, until softened. Remove from the heat and let the garlic steep for another 2 minutes.

In a food processor, combine the goat cheese, Parmigiano Reggiano, cream cheese, walnuts, rosemary, black pepper, hot pepper, and salt. Whirl to mix.

Add the garlic and oil, and with the machine on, slowly drizzle in the pasta water. Blend to desired consistency. Season with additional salt, if needed.

¼ cup (60 ml) extra-virgin olive oil

2 large cloves garlic, halved lengthwise

4 ounces (112 g) fresh white goat cheese

¼ cup (25 g) grated Parmigiano Reggiano

2 tablespoons (28 g) cream cheese

¾ cup (75 g) walnut pieces

1 tablespoon chopped fresh rosemary

½ teaspoon coarsely cracked black pepper

¼ teaspoon crushed hot red pepper

¼ teaspoon coarse salt, or more to taste

½ cup (120 ml) hot pasta water or plain hot water

With jarred roasted red peppers, this piquant pesto comes together in a flash. Since both the almonds and garlic can turn from toasted to bitter in seconds, pay attention for the first 5 minutes. For lunch or as a first course, allow 2 ounces (55 g) uncooked spaghetti and ¼ cup (60 ml) pesto per serving. Toss the pasta with just enough pesto to coat and dollop the remainder on top. Pass extra cheese on the side. This pesto keeps well in a closed container in the refrigerator for at least 3 days.

# Toasted Almond and Roasted Red Pepper Pesto

MAKES ABOUT 1½ CUPS (360 ML)

⅓ cup (80 ml) extra-virgin olive oil

5 cloves garlic (4 thickly sliced lengthwise, 1 coarsely chopped)

⅓ cup (50 g) slivered almonds

¾ cup (115 g) coarsely diced roasted red peppers

2 tablespoons torn fresh basil leaves

2 teaspoons fresh lemon juice

1 teaspoon balsamic vinegar

¼ teaspoon salt

¼ teaspoon crushed hot red pepper, or more to taste

2 tablespoons grated Parmigiano Reggiano and/or pecorino Romano, plus more for the table

⅓ cup (80 ml) hot pasta water or plain water, or lightly salted plain water

In a small heavy saucepan, warm the oil over medium heat until it begins to bubble. Reduce the heat to medium-low. Add the 4 sliced garlic cloves to the hot oil and cook until they are just golden brown around the edges, about 3 minutes. Remove the garlic to a small bowl.

Add the almonds to the hot oil and cook until they are very lightly toasted, about 2 minutes. Remove the nuts when they are barely darker than beige; they will continue to cook. Add to the garlic. Let the oil cool slightly.

In a blender or food processor, combine the roasted peppers, remaining clove of raw garlic, roasted garlic and almonds, basil, lemon juice, vinegar, salt, hot pepper, and 2 tablespoons grated cheese along with the water. Blend until everything is finely chopped.

Because the mint will darken upon standing, as well as lose its aromatic quality, this pesto is best served soon after it is made. Not a problem since it takes about 5 minutes to throw together. The sauce clings well to a long, thin pasta, such as spaghettini. Cheese at the table is optional.

# Smoky Almond–Mint Pesto

MAKES ABOUT 1½ CUPS (360 ML)

In a food processor, combine the fresh mint, dried mint, smoked almonds, natural almonds, and olive oil. Pulse until the mint and nuts are coarsely chopped. Add the cream cheese, pasta water, and a generous grind of black pepper. Whirl briefly to blend.

2 cups fresh mint leaves, from about 2 bunches mint (40 g)

2 teaspoons dried spearmint

¾ cup (7½ ounces/285 g) smoked almonds (seasoned are fine)

½ cup (5 ounces/190 g) fresh natural almonds

⅓ cup (80 ml) extra-virgin olive oil

2 tablespoons cream cheese

⅔ cup (160 ml) hot pasta water or plain water

Freshly ground black pepper

Packaged, prewashed baby arugula lets you easily whip up a pungent pesto. If you don't have pine nuts, substitute slivered almonds. This amount of pesto will sauce 8 ounces (225 g) of pasta, enough for four as a first course or two as a vegetarian main dish. For the pasta water, if you're not boiling the pasta while you make the pesto, use plain water plus a little salt.

# Arugula and Toasted Pine Nut Pesto

MAKES ABOUT 1½ CUPS (360 ML)

Put the arugula in a blender or food processor. In a small heavy saucepan, warm the olive oil over medium heat. Add the nuts, reduce the heat to low, and toast until they are very light brown, 2 to 3 minutes. Pour the nuts and hot oil over the arugula.

Add the garlic and hot pepper. Pulse to a coarse puree. Mix in the cheese. Add the pasta water and puree to a saucy consistency. Season with salt and black pepper.

5 ounces (140 g) baby arugula

⅓ cup (80 ml) extra-virgin olive oil

½ cup (70 g) pine nuts

2 cloves garlic, crushed through a press

¼ teaspoon crushed hot red pepper

½ cup (50 g) grated pecorino Romano

⅔ cup (160 ml) pasta water, or more if needed

Coarse salt and freshly ground black pepper

Fragrant *agrumi*, citrus, marries well with simple seafood pastas such as crab, sautéed halibut, sole, and shrimp. The tangy citrus wakes up grilled chicken, too. Mix this with ½ cup (115 g) of cream cheese for a super dip. This generously dresses 12 to 14 ounces (340 to 400 g) of pasta. It doubles easily, but it's assertive, so this small amount is usually sufficient.

# Sicilian Citrus Pesto

MAKES ABOUT 1 CUP (240 ML)

2 cups (40 g) lightly packed fresh basil leaves

2 cloves garlic, quartered

¼ teaspoon coarse salt

3 tablespoons fresh orange juice

2 tablespoons fresh lemon juice

1 tablespoon fresh lime juice

2 tablespoons sliced almonds

3 tablespoons extra-virgin olive oil

½ cup (50 g) grated Parmigiano Reggiano or pecorino Toscana

In a food processor, combine the basil, garlic, salt, orange juice, lemon juice, lime juice, and almonds. Pulse 4 or 5 times. Then, with the machine on, add the olive oil, then the cheese. Scrape down the inside of the processor with a spatula. Pulse about 10 times, until the pesto is coarsely chopped.

A garlic scape is the bright green stalk and flower bud of the garlic plant. Find them in farmers' markets and some produce stores in the spring and summer, where they are usually sold in small bunches. Two or three, combined with a small bunch of basil, are plenty for a pesto. Their advantage, besides the color, is the distinct flavor they impart, with no harsh bite. For best consistency, use the flower bud and the tender top few inches of the stalk. This amount sauces 8 ounces (225 g) of pasta and is best used the same day it's made.

# Garlic Scape Pesto

MAKES ABOUT 1½ CUPS (360 ML)

In a blender or food processor, combine the garlic scapes, basil, cream cheese, salt, and pepper. Puree until almost smooth.

With the machine on, slowly pour in the olive oil and then the hot water to make an emulsion. Add the Parmigiano and blend just until mixed.

2 or 3 large garlic scapes, bud and top 3 inches (7.5 cm) of stem cut into 1-inch (2.5 cm) lengths

1½ cups (30 g) lightly packed fresh basil leaves

2 tablespoons cream cheese

¼ teaspoon coarse salt

¼ teaspoon coarsely ground black pepper

⅓ cup (80 ml) extra-virgin olive oil

¾ cup (180 ml) hot pasta water or plain hot water

½ cup (50 g) grated Parmigiano Reggiano

The inspiration for this pesto came from our photographer, Steven Rothfeld, a long-time vegetarian. Kale is such a healthy vegetable and so popular, but it's nice to have another way of using it beyond salad and roasted chips. The type of kale called "lacinato," or "dinosaur," is an essential ingredient in Tuscany's great *ribollita* soup. This recipe makes enough pesto to sauce 8 ounces (225 g) of pasta. It doubles perfectly and keeps well for up to 3 days.

# Kale and Pistachio Pesto

MAKES 1½ CUPS (360 ML)

Bring a large pot of boiling salted water to a boil. Add the kale and cook, stirring once or twice, until the kale is tender but still bright green, 2 to 3 minutes. Scoop out and reserve ½ cup (120 ml) of the pasta water. Drain the kale into a colander and rinse briefly under cold water. Press gently to remove excess water. Transfer to a blender or food processor and pulse to chop coarsely.

In a small saucepan, combine the olive oil with the garlic. Cook over medium-low heat until the garlic is golden, 2 to 3 minutes.

Add the garlic and olive oil, pistachios, and hot pepper to the kale. Process to a coarse puree. With the machine on, gradually add the pasta water, blending to a thick paste. Add the cheese and process enough to mix. Season with salt and black pepper.

———

NOTE: Bunches of kale vary in size, which is why the recipe calls for a weight. To remove tough stems, simply fold the leaf in half lengthwise with one hand so the ribbed side is up. With your other hand, grasp the end of the stem and pull up. It will come right off. Any stem that remains is tender enough to cook.

1 bunch (8 ounces/225 g) kale, tough stems removed, leaves cut roughly into 2- to 3-inch (5 to 7.5 cm) lengths (see Note)

¼ cup (60 ml) extra-virgin olive oil

3 cloves garlic, peeled and smashed

2 tablespoons (1 ounce/ 28 g) shelled pistachios, coarsely chopped

¼ teaspoon crushed hot red pepper

½ cup (120 ml) hot pasta water or plain hot water

½ cup (50 g) grated Parmigiano Reggiano and/ or pecorino Romano

Coarse salt and freshly ground black pepper

This pesto is almost instantaneous to make, and the double dose of olive—the fruit and the oil—lends a soul-of-Italy flavor to a plain plate of spaghetti. The recipe makes enough to sauce 12 ounces (340 g) of pasta—just top with more cheese. It's also good at drinks time as a crostini spread. It keeps well in the fridge for a week.

# Olive Pesto

MAKES ABOUT 2 CUPS (480 ML)

2 tablespoons (1 ounce/ 25 g) pine nuts

2 cloves garlic, quartered

2 cups (280 g) pitted brined black or green olives, or a mix

½ cup (20 g) chopped fresh flat-leaf parsley

1 teaspoon fresh thyme leaves, or ½ teaspoon dried

¼ teaspoon crushed hot red pepper

½ cup (120 ml) extra-virgin olive oil

¼ cup (25 g) grated Parmigiano Reggiano or pecorino Toscana

In a food processor, pulse the pine nuts and garlic 3 or 4 times, then add the olives, parsley, thyme, and hot pepper. Pulse until coarsely chopped. With the machine on, slowly pour in the oil in a stream until mixed. Add the cheese and pulse 6 or 7 times, until well incorporated.

Rich *salsa di noci* is cherished all over Italy. Of all nuts, walnuts are the preferred, with pistachios, hazelnuts, and pine nuts close behind. Dessert is often a fig and walnut tart, but after dinner, guests may linger over a handful of nuts, some tangerines, and a hunk of aged pecorino. Here, a few pine nuts are added for a hint of sweetness. This recipe easily sauces 8 ounces (225 g) of pasta. This is a Ligurian specialty, so the local trofie pasta is the traditional choice. *Casarecce* or *torchietti* also work well. Plan to use the whole amount, as this doesn't store well. Any leftover walnut pesto is good on crostini for the antipasto platter. Consider ending the dinner with the spicy walnut *digestivo* called *nocino*.

# Walnut Pesto

MAKES ABOUT 1½ CUPS (360 ML)

Place the breadcrumbs and milk in a food processor and let them soak for a minute or two until the bread softens. Add the garlic, walnuts, pine nuts, and salt. Process by pulsing—about 8 times—while drizzling in the olive oil. The nuts should look finely chopped but not pulverized. Add the Parmigiano and pulse about 4 times to mix. Add a little more Parmigiano if the pesto seems too soft, a little more olive oil if it seems too dense. It should have the consistency of ricotta. When adding this pesto to pasta, the thick consistency should be just right, but if you like, use 2 or 3 tablespoons pasta water to obtain a creamier texture. Garnish with the fresh herbs.

¼ cup (25 g) breadcrumbs

1 cup (240 ml) whole milk

1 clove garlic, quartered

¾ cup (90 g) shelled fresh walnuts

1 tablespoon pine nuts

¼ teaspoon coarse salt

2 tablespoons extra-virgin olive oil, plus more if needed

¼ cup (25 g) grated Parmigiano Reggiano, plus more if needed

Fresh thyme sprigs or sage leaves, for garnish

# Resources

When ingredients mentioned in these recipes aren't readily available in local markets, online shopping is the easy solution. Although a range of pasta choices in our supermarkets is common now, to enjoy ruote, torchietti, mezze maniche, cavatappi, bronze-cut pastas, and the many others suggested in *Pasta Veloce*, you're only a click away from overnight delivery. Order five or six types at a time, and stock your shelves.

Some good online sources for quality Italian pastas are Eataly, which is associated with Slow Foods, Gustiamo, Market Hall Foods, Italian Foods Online, and Delallo. And, of course, all you have to do is google a shape to try to find it. Amazon offers a huge range of brands made in Italy.

Many of the same companies sell Italian *salume*, as well. Fortuna Sausage offers excellent salamis as well as a wide range of pasta shapes, truffle oil, cheeses, and many other Italian products. D'Artagnan produces a fine duck confit, available online and in some supermarkets. They also sell white truffle oil. The Mozzarella Company out of Dallas makes authentic mozzarellas.

Some recipes call for other items your market may not have: preserved lemon (aka lemon confit), rosemary dust, fennel pollen, dried porcini, chili crisp, scarmorza, and other cheeses. Find them easily online.

# Acknowledgments

First thanks go to Edward Mayes. He tasted, cooked, shopped, loaded the dishwasher, upped the hot red pepper in many recipes, shopped again, proofed recipes, opened bottles of wine, and never wavered in his enthusiasm for yet another plate of pasta. His once-stated desire to eat a different pasta every day of the year partly engendered this book. Edoardo, a laurel crown for you.

*Mille grazie* to Susan Gravely, founder of Vietri Inc., importers and designers of distinctive Italian tableware, and to Busatti's Sassolini family—Giovanni, Paola, Livio, Stefano—and Michelangelo Formica, makers of Busatti's stupendous Tuscan fabrics in both traditional and innovative designs for eight generations. These great friends enhance the homes of hundreds of thousands with their inspired designs. They generously shared their unique products for our photography, allowing us exciting choices to complement the pastas. Vietri's imaginative flatware, glasses, plates, and platters bring joy to many, many pages of our book. The natural colors of Tuscany found in Busatti's fabled tablecloths, napkins, placemats, and runners are never just background but easily assert their charms and flair. We love you and thank you!

Cortona friends and exceptional cooks Gilda Di Vizio and Coco Pante opened their cupboards to us as well. Many thanks for serving pieces, plates, and vintage table linens. We had fun with such a variety to choose from.

Silvia Regi Baracchi, super chef, is such a dazzling presence in the kitchen. We thank her for two of her creative, original recipes and for gracious dinners at her sybaritic inn, Il Falconieri, in her vineyards near Cortona.

We are so grateful to Laura Dozier, our astute editor at Abrams, and to the book designers Diane Shaw and Annie Marino, all of whom brought

Tuscan light onto the pages. We love the joyous invitation to cook! Thanks also to Asha Simon, Mike Richards, Kathleen Gaffney, Natasha Martin, Danielle Kolodkin, and Mamie VanLangen.

It's always a pleasure to work with perfectionist photographer Steven Rothfeld, who also loves to invent recipes. A consummate traveler, Steven has photographed most square inches of Italy. This time we had the added pleasure of working with his talented wife, Susan Swan, who kept us all in line and the music playing.

Our agent, Peter Ginsberg of Curtis Brown Ltd., is a superhero, as well as being always fun to talk to. We could not be in better hands.

It's too easy to love your own recipes, so we feel lucky, lucky to have wonderful friends and family who enthusiastically pulled up their chairs and tasted our works in progress, often providing valuable feedback. We feasted and stayed late to toast. Here goes another cin cin to Ashley King, Peter Leousis, Will King, Maureen Quilligan, Michael Malone, Fred Stewart, Jimmy Holcomb, Elizabeth Woodman, Eric Hallman, Steven Burke, Randy Campbell, Elizabeth Matheson, Tori Reynolds, John Beerman, Allan Gurganus, Jane Holding, Lee Smith, Hal Crowther, Karen and Doug Clark, Khatoon Noorani, Ray McArthur, Gale and Geoff Greene, Ippy and Neil Patterson, Ann Stewart, Randall Roden, Francesca Talenti, Pier Carlo Talenti, Coco and Jim Pante, Fulvio and Aurora Di Rosa, Gilda Di Vizio, Susie and Rowan Russell, Nora Holley, Mike MacMillan, Susan Gladin, and Michael Patrick.

Special thanks to the Cardinale family, at whose bountiful table Frances and Ed still learn so much about Tuscan cooking.

# Index

Note: Page numbers in *italics* indicate photos. Page numbers in **bold** indicate pasta variety descriptions and illustrations.

Editor: Laura Dozier

Managing Editor: Mike Richards

Designer: Annie Marino

Design Manager: Danny Maloney

Illustrations pages 22–26 and endpapers: Jenice Kim

Production Manager: Kathleen Gaffney

Library of Congress Control Number: 2022944494

ISBN: 978-1-4197-6314-4

eISBN: 978-1-64700-747-8

Printed and bound in China

10 9 8 7 6 5 4 3 2 1

Abrams books are available at special discounts when purchased in quantity for premiums and promotions as well as fundraising or educational use. Special editions can also be created to specification. For details, contact specialsales@abramsbooks.com or the address below.

Abrams® is a registered trademark of Harry N. Abrams, Inc.

**ABRAMS** The Art of Books
195 Broadway, New York, NY 10007
abramsbooks.com